The Generous Wife

~ A Year of Generous Tips ~

The Generous Wife

~ A Year of Generous Tips ~

LORI BYERLY
Co-Creator of The Marriage Bed

Karis Publishing
Austin, TX

THE GENEROUS WIFE
A Year of Generous Tips

Cover art by: Lori Byerly

Published in Austin, TX, by Karis Publishing, Inc.

Karis Publishing, Inc.
1019 Meredith Drive
Austin, TX 78748 USA

ISBN: 0-9718040-4-4

This book is dedicated to:

The Gentleman on My Right

the man who loves me as I am
who brings me lots of
root beer and chocolate

Table of Contents

Acknowledgements

God gave me breath and the ideas and ability to be generous. He gets all the credit.

I'd like to thank Him for my generous husband, kids that any parent would be proud to own up to, and many great friends who have prayed for this book (special thanks to the church at Kurtis and Lisa's house, TMB prayer warriors, and Felicity) and patiently edited it's pages (thanks Alise and Jason). You have all blessed me with your generosity and caring.

Love y'all, Lori <><

Forward

The Generous Wife - quite a label to live up to. I suppose the reader might wonder if Lori practices what she preaches, if she really is the generous wife. As her husband I think I am qualified to answer those questions with a resounding yes!!

I remember when Lori told me that her Bible reading and prayer time had lead her to the conclusion that Christians should be very generous. She decided that real generosity required giving what people most wanted and needed. She also decided that one must first and foremost be generous to their family. By the time Lori discussed this with me she had already begun to live it, and I was aware of her growing generosity towards our children and me.

For many years, I've been impressed by, and blessed by, my wife's generosity. I've also been humbled and challenged. My response to her increased generosity has been to repay her in kind, and to carry it beyond our relationship. I know that Lori did not sow generosity to reap the same; I also know that such a harvest is a Biblically predicted result of her actions.

Yes, Lori is THE generous wife. I believe that what she has become is worthy of emulating, and I know that any man would be blessed to have his wife follow her example.

~ Paul H. Byerly

Her children rise up and bless her;
Her husband also, and he praises her,
saying: Many daughters have done
nobly, But you excel them all.
Proverbs 31:28-29

Introduction

The Generous Wife tips came out of my own search to understand how to build my marriage. I had seen so many failed marriages and my husband and I were struggling in ours.

I knew what not to do, but I wasn't sure what to do. I started by stopping anything that didn't work, which meant I didn't do a whole lot at first, but then gradually I began to realize that doing something nice regardless of the circumstances improved the atmosphere of my home. I began to practice different attitudes and actions, and this began to have a real impact. Eventually I called it "being generous" because really it was a choice I made to be generous in speech and action, a gift to those around me.

Later God led me to share the tips by email. Given my background in marriage ministry and specifically in the area of sexuality, I did build in a healthy emphasis on being sexually generous. Sexuality is an integral part of people, and men, in particular, have a strong need to be affirmed sexually. It's also fairly common for women to need some ideas and a little encouragement where the bedroom is concerned.

Please note that I tend to type as I speak, you will find the occasional Texan term (I've lived in Texas for over 20 years and the colorful language eventually creeps in). My most humble apologies to English teachers everywhere.

For your benefit, I offer the following glossary of terms.

♥ critter - animal, can be used as an affectionate term for a husband

♥ gopher – furry critter that digs up your garden, one who helps out ("go fer this," "go fer that")

♥ gussied up – dressed up, fancied up

♥ 'fess up – tell the truth

♥ folk – regular people

♥ messin' with – touching, getting into

♥ y'all – contraction of the words "you all"

How to Use This Book

The Generous Wife is offered as a pool of ideas, a source of creative material for your marriage. The tips are designed to help you build intimacy and fun within your marriage. They are set up so that you can read them by day of the week or day of the year. You can also just use the book as a general source for ideas, reading when you have the time and energy to do something fun for your husband.

Here are some additional suggestions:

♥ Personalize the Tips

We all have different marriage relationships and the tips can be used a number of ways. For example, if I suggest that you give your husband a shoulder massage when he comes home from work and your husband works at home, then consider giving him a shoulder massage when you know he's been sitting at his desk for a long time or after coming in from doing some yard work. The idea is that you give him a little physical attention and relief from muscle pain. You know your husband; you pick the time and place.

♡ Know Your Husband

Some tips are really going to bless your husband
and others might not. If your husband doesn't like
people messin' with his clothes then please don't
follow the "fix up his wardrobe" tip. Instead, buy
him a new shirt or just compliment him on how
nice he looks. The idea is to build him up by
doing something for his appearance/clothes. You
know your husband; you pick how to express the
idea behind the tip.

♡ Bless Intentionally

Pay special attention to the tips that speak to your
husband's likes and needs. If he loves to spend
time with you, then pay closer attention to the tips
that offer ideas for quality time with him.

♡ You Don't Have to Do Every Tip, Every Day!

The Generous Wife tips are designed to jog your
thinking everyday. They are there to remind you
to bless your husband and to give you a variety of
ideas to use. I would guess that most of us don't
have the time to do every tip, every day (but it

would certainly be fun to try!). Please take the ideas that will work for you; that you have the time, money, and energy for, and bless your husband's socks off.

♥ When the Tip Just Won't Work

Of course, there will be some tips that will be totally unsuitable for your marriage. If it's just about personal taste, not a problem, just skip the tip. If it's an area of struggle for the two of you, use that day to pray for that area of your relationship. For example, if you are married to an unbeliever, your husband might not be blessed by having you "hug and pray for him when he's struggling." Instead, pray quietly by yourself over your husband's struggles. Ask the Lord to grow a developing hunger in your husband for God.

♥ Please Use Common Sense

Please think things through so that you do not upset, embarrass, or harm your husband (hanging from the chandelier really can be dangerous!)

♥ Get Help When You Need It

If you are in an abusive marriage, please get help now.   No amount of generosity will help in a situation where your life or wellbeing is at risk.

National Abuse Hotline: 1-800-799-7233

If you and your husband are having significant marriage difficulties, please seek help.   Talk to your minister or ask a trusted friend for a referral to a counselor that they respect.

Online resource: http://www.aacc.net
(Click on the "find a counselor" link at the top of the page.)

A Year of Generous Tips

SUNDAY   JANUARY 1
-♡-

Pray for your husband to have a healthy, balanced self-image. So much in life can tear you down or falsely build you up. He needs to know his worth in Christ and be able to like himself as he was created.

MONDAY   JANUARY 2
-♡-

Frame a fun picture of the two of you for your bedroom nightstand or wall. Remembering special moments builds intimacy.

TUESDAY   JANUARY 3
-♡-

Look for opportunities to compliment your husband in front of others (moderate bragging is allowed). If he is there to hear your words, he will be blessed. If he hears them later second hand, imagine how great he will feel to hear that you've been saying nice things about him to other people!

WEDNESDAY   JANUARY 4

-♡-

Play "toll booth" in a doorway. Your husband can't get by you until he "pays with a kiss" (or other "penalty").

Your lips, my bride, drip honey;
Honey and milk are under your tongue ...
Song of Songs 4:11a

THURSDAY   JANUARY 5

-♡-

Help your husband with his diet. Whether it's a normal balanced diet, high protein, low fat, or low carb, keep those needs in mind when planning meals and snacks

FRIDAY   JANUARY 6

-♡-

Develop a common interest, perhaps a new sport or maybe a new area of study. Whatever you do, it will give the two of you regular, fun time together.

SATURDAY   JANUARY 7

-♡-

Doing something unexpected can make your intimate life more interesting. Look for an unusual time of day or night to initiate sex. If you usually make love at bedtime, try in the morning or even in the middle of the night. If it's usually in the morning, try just before dinner or during the afternoon on a day off.

The New Year

New Year's Day (or any other time of "new beginnings") offers a unique opportunity to bless your spouse. Spend time talking and praying with your husband about direction and change for the new year.

♡♡♡♡♡

Ask questions like, "What can we do to make our marriage stronger?" or "Do we have a united vision of what our marriage should look like?" Look critically at your priorities and at how you both spend your time. Are there things that need to change? Even small changes can have a large effect over time.

♡♡♡♡♡

This is also a time to offer practical help. Offer to mark any of his calendars with birthdays, anniversaries, and any other special days that he likes to celebrate. Is there an area of the house that needs cleaning up and organizing to make it more functional for home or business needs? Do either of you need to rethink or exchange any household responsibilities?

New Year's Resolutions ...

We all know that most resolutions are rarely kept, but I think this is largely because they are often unrealistic or overcomplicated. This year make small, attainable resolutions. How are your attitudes and actions toward your spouse? What one thing can you change and practice until it becomes habit?

A few generous suggestions ...

♡ Pay attention to your husband when he speaks and practice responding with a kind tone of voice.

♡ Develop the touch habit. When you walk by your husband, touch him in some way ... a soft kiss on the ear, a squeeze of his shoulder, or a pat on the arm (or wherever).

♡ Compliment him or thank him daily. It doesn't have to be much, just a "you look nice" or "thanks for taking out the trash." It will not only build him up, it will help you stay aware of his strengths and kindnesses.

If you falter now and then, don't let it get you off track. Just take a deep breath and start again.

SUNDAY   JANUARY 8

-♡-

Pray for a growing sense of trust and emotional intimacy in your marriage.

♡♡♡♡♡

MONDAY   JANUARY 9

-♡-

Write out several different quotes about love on postcards and mail them to your sweetie one a day (be sure to decorate them with stickers and give them a light spray of perfume). Check your concordance for love scriptures or head for the library to check out a quotation book (you can also check out quotation sites online).

TUESDAY   JANUARY 10

-♡-

Here's a question to ask your husband sometime when you really have his attention. "What can I do to be a more supportive wife?"

WEDNESDAY   JANUARY 11
-♡-

Keep an eye open for marriage enrichment
seminars or retreats in your area. There's nothing
like a little "continuing education" to keep the
flames burning bright.

... be ready for every good deed.
Titus 3:1b

THURSDAY   JANUARY 12
-♡-

Is there something hanging over your husband's
head that needs to be done, and he's putting it off
because he doesn't feel up to taking care of it?
Be a sport and help him out. Is the messy garage
calling his name? Pull on your work clothes and
work elbow to elbow with him. Does he have a
zillion errands to run? Hop in the car with him
and make it an enjoyable time instead of drudgery
(be sure to stop for a sundae and play with his
feet under the table). Think creative and be a
help.

FRIDAY   JANUARY 13

-♡-

Buy matching items for your husband and yourself. It could be T-shirts, coffee mugs or anything. Just make the statement that you are a couple.

SATURDAY   JANUARY 14

-♡-

One of the kindest and most loving things you can do for your husband is to create an atmosphere of acceptance when it comes to his sexuality. When your husband gets a little frisky, as often as possible, choose to get frisky right back.

SUNDAY   JANUARY 15

-♡-

Pray for your husband to have discernment and wisdom.

MONDAY   JANUARY 16

-♡-

Kiss him at a stoplight.

TUESDAY   JANUARY 17

-♡-

When your husband is working outside or working on a household project, baby him a little. Take him a drink, give him a little help, and be sure to tell him what a wonderful job he's doing.

WEDNESDAY   JANUARY 18

-♡-

Take a little time to clean up and straighten your bedroom. Are there piles of laundry lying around? Not very romantic. Fold them and put them away. Piles of papers? Sort and file them. Straighten up, here a bit and there a bit. Put fresh sheets on the bed and set out a candle or two. Make your bedroom that special room for just the two of you, where you can talk, share, and love.

THURSDAY   JANUARY 19

-♡-

Next time you go to the store, buy his favorite ice cream. Vanilla? Chocolate? Candy Bar Classic? If he's on a diet look for a new low calorie treat to try.

FRIDAY   JANUARY 20

-♡-

Call your husband at lunchtime (or when you know he has a break), just to share your day and tell him how special he is to you.

SATURDAY   JANUARY 21

-♡-

Don't be afraid to be yourself in the bedroom. Ask for what you think you would like. Be a little spontaneous. Don't be concerned about how you look or sound. Allow your husband to see a more private and personal side of you.

But my dove, my perfect one,
is unique ...
Song of Songs 6:9a

Prayer

It cannot be overstated how important prayer is to the health of your marriage. We are in a spiritual battle and our husbands and marriages are under attack from the enemy. I encourage you to set aside time *daily* to keep your husband and your marriage in prayer.

♡♡♡♡♡

Some helpful suggestions ...

♡ Keep a prayer journal.

As you pray each day, write down your prayers. What you write will stand as a reminder to carry certain people and situations to God in prayer each day. Also, as the Lord answers your prayers, make note of it in your prayer journal. You'll have a wonderful tool to help you stay faithful to pray, and also a record of God's faithfulness in responding to your prayers.

♥ Get a prayer partner or two.

This can be your husband, a good friend, or both. Regularly pray together and encourage each other. Gather over coffee, over the phone, or by email.

♥ Study and meditate on the Word.

Knowing what God says about prayer will help you stand in faith as you pray. Add your study notes to your prayer journal.

♥ Read good books on prayer.

Learn from the writings of other believers. Books like *The Power of a Praying Wife* by Stormie Omartian can offer fresh insight and motivation to pray. Be sure to add any insights gained in your prayer journal.

The effective prayer of a righteous [wo]man can accomplish much.
James 5:16

SUNDAY   JANUARY 22

-♥-

Pray for your husband's friendships. We all need supportive, encouraging, same sex friends. Pray that God would use his current friends to build him up and bless him or that God would draw new godly friends to him.

♥♥♥♥♥

MONDAY   JANUARY 23

-♥-

Buy some romantic stickers (hearts, I love you's, etc.). You can use them in the traditional way on notes or romantic cards. You can also use them as little symbols of love, like leaving a little heart on his steering wheel or on the bathroom mirror.

TUESDAY   JANUARY 24

-♥-

In a group setting, show preference to your husband - listen to him, serve him, sit next to him, speak well of him, etc.

WEDNESDAY   JANUARY 25

-♡-

Take the time to find a really nice perfume, cologne, or body wash. Your husband will eventually associate that lovely smell with you. When you walk by or lean over and kiss him, he will find it to be a pleasant enticement.

THURSDAY   JANUARY 26

-♡-

What happens first thing in the morning can set the tone for a person's whole day. Make sure that your early morning conversation with your husband is kind and encouraging.

♡♡♡♡♡

FRIDAY   JANUARY 27

-♡-

Invite your husband for a walk. Talk about anything or nothing. Hold his hand or loop your arm through his. Look at the clouds in the sky, the kids riding their bikes, or the neighbor's flower garden.

SATURDAY   JANUARY 28

-♥-

Undress him. Take your time and be sure to use your hands and lips to arouse and delight. If he wants to return the favor, why not let him?

SUNDAY   JANUARY 29

-♥-

Pray for your husband's health and general physical condition.

***I pray that ... you may prosper
and be in good health ...***
3 John 2

MONDAY   JANUARY 30

-♥-

Create your own romantic rituals. It might be as simple as kissing goodbye each morning or as elaborate as a yearly cruise getaway. The idea is that you do something that is unique to the two of you on a regular basis. (Other ideas: reading the newspaper in bed together on the weekend, meeting for lunch on Thursdays, regularly taking a walk after dinner, a monthly or weekly date night, showering together each evening, or spending ten minutes each morning just cuddling before you get up.)

TUESDAY   JANUARY 31

-♡-

Sometimes a little gift will cheer up a person. Find a hiding place (like your sewing drawer or a box on a high shelf) to tuck a few small gifts to have on hand for your husband. When you think he needs a little cheering up, pick out a gift, run up to him, give him a big hug and kiss, and hand him the gift.

WEDNESDAY   FEBRUARY 1

-♡-

Write a little note and tuck it in your husband's lunchbox, wallet, whatever (some place where he will find it during the day). Tell him how much you want him and what you are going to do to him when he gets home.

THURSDAY   FEBRUARY 2

-♡-

Give your husband a scalp massage. It's relaxing, soothing, and a kind thing to do for him after a busy day.

FRIDAY   FEBRUARY 3

-♡-

Share something that you recently read in a newspaper, magazine, or book

May my beloved come into his garden,
And eat its choice fruits!
Song of Songs 4:16b

SATURDAY   FEBRUARY 4

-♡-

Ask your husband to help you with a project in another room. The project is your "stuck" zipper or "difficult" bra clasp.

Valentine's Day

(and other romantic holidays)

Valentine's Day is a time for romance! Silly romance! Serious romance! Sexy romance! Go all out to let your husband know that he is your one and only valentine.

♡ Cards

There are all kinds of cards from silly to romantic, store bought to homemade. Consider delivery (by mail, left on his pillow with a ribbon, hand delivered by a friend, etc.) and consider quantity (one or two very special cards or lots and lots of cards - you could even leave him dozens of silly kid's valentines everywhere). There are quite a few options. What will make your husband feel the most special?

♡♡♡♡♡

Just an aside ... take advantage of after Valentine's Day sales. There are stickers, cards, lingerie, etc. that could be used the rest of the year.

♥Gifts

Consider romantic type gifts like a framed picture of the two of you. And, of course, you can never go wrong with chocolate (especially if he is the sharing type).

♥ Dates

If your husband hasn't already covered this, invite him out! Go somewhere new or go somewhere associated with fond memories. If you have a little extra in the bank, you might want to plan a romantic getaway complete with hotel and a hot tub. If finances are a little tight, have a candlelit dinner and movie at home (swap baby-sitting with a friend so you can each have a night alone with your own husband).

♥ Words

Don't forget to tell your husband that you love him. Get creative and tell him in as many ways as you can. Leave a sexy note on the bathroom mirror or send an email. Call him at work or leave a message for him on his answering machine.

♡ Touch

Give him lots of hugs and kisses. Hold his hand or loop your arm through his. If sex is an area of tension in the marriage, I encourage you to invite him into the bedroom for a little intimate time before any evening plans. Your husband will be blessed and you can both relax and enjoy the evening knowing that being tired later won't be a problem.

How do I love thee,
let me count the ways ...
Elizabeth Barrett Browning

SUNDAY   FEBRUARY 5
-♡-

Pray for your husband to have a sense of fulfillment at work.

MONDAY   FEBRUARY 6
-♡-

Buy a heart keychain, tie tack, or other man's item for your husband to remind him of your love.

TUESDAY   FEBRUARY 7
-♡-

We are all individuals with our own unique gifts and abilities. Take the time to encourage your husband to develop his abilities and skills.

WEDNESDAY   FEBRUARY 8
-♡-

One of the nicest things you can do is to be accepting and appreciative of your husband's body. So touch, stroke, tug, tickle, and kiss. Let him know how much you appreciate every square inch of him.

THURSDAY   FEBRUARY 9

Is there a spot in the house that just doesn't work for your husband? Maybe it's the drop off spot by the front door or maybe it's the bedroom closet. Wherever it is, take the time to pray about it and consider how things could be arranged more conveniently for him.

... through love serve one another.
Galatians 5:13b

FRIDAY   FEBRUARY 10

Simplify your life so that you have time for each other. Do you really need to watch every rerun of *Friends* or be on 14 committees? Give up the less important for the more important. Make time for each other.

SATURDAY   FEBRUARY 11

-♡-

Invite your husband into the shower with you for a sensuous time of shared pleasure. Take the time to wash each other and explore those long forgotten spots or new unexplored ones. Don't forget a couple of soft washcloths and a gently scented bar of soap.

♡♡♡♡♡

SUNDAY   FEBRUARY 12

-♡-

Pray for those areas of your husband's life where he has struggles. Perhaps it's an attitude or a habit. Maybe it's a relationship or a responsibility. Whatever it is, lift him up in prayer.

♡♡♡♡♡

MONDAY   FEBRUARY 13

-♡-

Tell your husband what first attracted you to him. If you've already told him, remind him again.

TUESDAY   FEBRUARY 14

-♥-

Write out a "profile" on your husband. Make it as detailed as you can. Is he an introvert? Extrovert? What are his favorite activities? Is he a neatnik or a messie? It helps to pretend as though you are writing a report for the FBI.

When you have it all written out, you should have a fairly accurate picture of whom he is. Pray over it and ask God to help you love and accept your husband for the wonderful individual that he is.

♥♥♥♥♥

WEDNESDAY   FEBRUARY 15

-♥-

Rethink your sexuality. It's very difficult to be sexual when you have thoughts like "good girls don't" or "sex is dirty." Ask yourself what God really says about sex and compare with how you view it. Need help in sorting things out? Check out *Intimate Issues* by Dillow and Pintus.

THURSDAY   FEBRUARY 16

-♡-

Next time you go to the movies (or rent one for home viewing), let your husband pick the flick.

♡♡♡♡♡

FRIDAY   FEBRUARY 17

-♡-

Buy your husband a pound or two of his favorite candy. It's a "sweet" way of doing something nice for your best friend.

♡♡♡♡♡

SATURDAY   FEBRUARY 18

-♡-

Want to try something a little fun? Get your kitchen timer and set it. Then tell your husband that he has that much time to do a bedroom activity of your choosing. Five minutes or fifty, I guarantee he'll enjoy the challenge.

Acceptance

One of the kindest things you can do is to be accepting of your husband. God designed him. He is a unique combination of gender, personality, life experience, and more. This is not to say that he is perfect or that you should ignore sin, but it is saying that his design was not a mistake, he doesn't need to change who he innately is, and he needs to be appreciated for who he is.

♡♡♡♡♡

♡ Gender

At a certain point during gestation, hormones are released that begin to change a baby according to gender. These changes create the outward physical differences between gender and they also affect how the brain develops. The brain is "feminized" or "masculinized" depending on what set of instructions it gets. Both male and female brains are capable of creativity and intelligence, but they may use different parts of the brain and each has unique strengths and abilities. As an example, this accounts for the typical male single-mindedness and the typical woman's ability to multi-task. These are general traits by gender (there are always individual exceptions).

Your husband is a "guy." Appreciate his strength, his single-mindedness, his hand-eye coordination, and don't ask him to stop for directions.

♥ Personality

He may be introverted or extroverted, laid-back or Type A personality. He may like order or creative clutter, crowds or solitude. We all have a natural bent. To make matters more challenging, it's very typical for opposite personality types to marry (something of an "opposites attract" equation). Read up a bit on personality types so that you can understand some of your husband's personality quirks and how they interact with your own.

♥ Strengths and Weaknesses

Along with his natural personality bent will come natural abilities and character strengths and, the flip side of the coin, his inabilities and weaknesses. These are all a part of the man you married.

Does he have a talent or two or three? Is he naturally patient or does he need encouragement to control his temper? Is he a gifted musician or mediator?

Encourage and praise his strengths and abilities, and cover his weaknesses and failings with understanding, wise encouragement, grace, and prayer.

♡ Life Experience

Our experiences greatly influence how we think and feel. In what kind of family did your husband grow up? What were his schooling years like? What kinds of relationships has he had? Work experiences? Has he experienced any trauma? Personal victories?

Know him for who he is. Love him for who he is.

*... **O you whom my soul loves** ...*
Song of Songs 1:7a

SUNDAY   FEBRUARY 19

-♡-

Pray for the ability to communicate well with your husband. Miscommunication and misunderstanding come along too easily. Pray for ease in working out those problems and working on good communication skills.

MONDAY   FEBRUARY 20

-♡-

How many times can you touch your husband in an evening (or day if you work evenings)? Stroke his arm as he walks by. Lean over and kiss him at his desk. Snuggle up against him while he reads or watches TV. Find a number of ways to tell him that you love him through touch.

TUESDAY   FEBRUARY 21

-♡-

Take a moment and look at the condition of your husbands clothes. Sew on a button, press something a bit here or there, or polish his shoes. He'll be blessed by your effort to make him look good.

WEDNESDAY   FEBRUARY 22

Ask your husband to pick out what he would like for you to wear on an evening out or even for an evening in.

THURSDAY   FEBRUARY 23

Look through your husband's things and replace anything that is worn out or used up (obvious exceptions would be anything with sentimental value).

... It is not good for the man to be alone;
I will make him a helper suitable for him.
Genesis 2:18

FRIDAY   FEBRUARY 24

Find a quiet moment to talk to your husband about how he envisions the ideal marriage. Talk about how you both can work toward that ideal.

SATURDAY   FEBRUARY 25
-♡-

Try making love with your clothes on (well, mostly).   It makes for a very passionate, spontaneous kind of lovemaking.

SUNDAY   FEBRUARY 26
-♡-

Pray for your husband's ability to be bold and courageous. Keeping a healthy Christian witness, leading the family, or being able to speak the truth in love can be pretty challenging some days, so support him with your prayers.

MONDAY   FEBRUARY 27
-♡-

Set aside regular time to be with your husband. Spend a few minutes together first thing in the morning, share meal times, and have regular dates. Find ways to spend time with each other over common interests. You are a couple and you need to have couple time together.

TUESDAY   FEBRUARY 28

Invite your husband to share his dreams and hopes with you. A lot of folks need to talk through their dreams to weed out the good from the goofy. How wonderful it is to be a part of that process, to encourage, listen, and learn more about his heart.

♡♡♡♡♡

WEDNESDAY   (for leap years) FEBRUARY 29

Make up some coupons for things that he likes you to do for him (in or out of the bedroom). Tuck them in his wallet, under his pillow, and in other interesting spots where he will find them (and the kids won't).

♡♡♡♡♡

THURSDAY   MARCH 1

Ask your husband, "What is the kindest thing I have ever done for you?" You might ask him about kind things that others have done for him as well. Listen and learn. You can tell a lot about what touches him the most.

... encourage the young women to
love their husbands ... to be ... kind ...
Titus 2:4-5

FRIDAY   MARCH 2
-♡-

Share a midnight snack (or a 10 o'clock snack if you are early birds). Take a few moments to connect over a treat before snuggling in for the night.

SATURDAY   MARCH 3
-♡-

Create a sexy treasure hunt. Leave a trail of clues where along the way he can pick up things like lubricant, condom (if you use one), massage oil, breath mints, etc. ... with you waiting in the bedroom as the treasure.

The Blessing of Generosity

I love Psalms and Proverbs. They are full of such wisdom and encouragement. Here are a few scriptures about the blessings that come from being generous. (I've changed the gender so that the scriptures will apply to all generous wives.)

The generous [wo]man will be prosperous, and [s]he who waters will [her]self be watered.
Proverbs 11:25

[S]he who is generous will be blessed ...
Proverbs 22:9a

Good will come to [her] who is generous ...
Psalms 112:5a NIV

You can't out give God. As He grows generosity in your heart and your life, blessings will flow your way.

SUNDAY   MARCH 4
-♡-

Pray for those who are your husband's "enemies," the one's who don't get along with him, the ones that are jealous of him, and the ones that are just down right angry at him (for real or imagined reasons). It's not easy, but we are commanded to love our enemies and pray for them. You will be sowing peace into a difficult situation.

But I say to you who hear, love your enemies, do good to those who hate you, bless those who curse you, pray for those who mistreat you.
Luke 6:27-28

MONDAY   MARCH 5
-♡-

Meet him for lunch somewhere - your favorite restaurant or share a bag lunch on a park bench. Just have a midday time together. Make a point of telling him how much you love him.

TUESDAY   MARCH 6

Take his "wants" seriously. Yes, I know, if he wants to buy one more CD or fishing lure, you might dissolve into a pool of tears, but please realize that (baring a serious addiction) the things that he wants are important to him, and in the long run are important to his emotional health. So smile the next time he mentions a "want" and maybe even go out and buy it for him.

WEDNESDAY   MARCH 7

Call him at work and say something REALLY sexy. Stretch yourself here. I realize that this may be a challenge for some, so here are a few ideas - "The kids are at grandma's house for a sleepover, and you're mine for the night!" "At 6:43 (or whatever appropriate time) I plan to be in bed (or wherever) wearing only my birthday suit," or "I've been thinking of you and I had to change my panties."

THURSDAY   MARCH 8

Get a subscription to his favorite magazine. If he doesn't have a favorite magazine, subscribe to one that is about his favorite interest or hobby.

FRIDAY   MARCH 9

Try singing in the shower together.

*Those who bring sunshine
to the lives of others cannot
keep it from themselves.*
Anonymous

SATURDAY   MARCH 10

Buy some stickers or rub-on tattoos and put them on your body in fun places. Or use a felt tip marker (the water-washable kind) and create a little body art. Draw hearts, kisses, arrows, etc. or write little love notes on portions of your body that only he will see (if you are the sensitive-skin type you may want to do a small test on your skin before you get too creative). Get dressed again (preferably in something with lots of buttons) and invite your husband to find your "artwork."

SUNDAY   MARCH 11

-♡-

Pray for financial wisdom for your husband.

MONDAY   MARCH 12

-♡-

Bake up a batch of his favorite cookies and have a friend deliver them to him at work with a note of love and appreciation for all that he does for you.

TUESDAY   MARCH 13
-♡-

Imagine that your words are seeds. When you speak to your husband plant seeds of acceptance, love, encouragement and honest praise. Just think what a wonderful garden you will have.

A word aptly spoken is like apples
of gold in settings of silver.
Proverbs 25:11 NIV

WEDNESDAY   MARCH 14
-♡-

Stroke yourself in front of him. It might be a simple stretch with your hand running across your breast or a blatant tease as you run a hand across your jeans (or his).

THURSDAY   MARCH 15

-♡-

Ask your husband if there is anything that you can do for him to make his day easier. I've done this frequently and it is always a kindness, even if there is nothing that needs to be done. It's just so nice to know that there's someone who cares about your day.

FRIDAY   MARCH 16

-♡-

When was the last time that you and your husband took on a project together? Do your flowerbeds need cleaning up? Does your church need a couple of teachers for a Bible study? Invite your husband to join you in a shared endeavor.

SATURDAY   MARCH 17

-♡-

Set a goal to make love in every room of the house in one month (or other appropriate time length - kids and number of rooms will play into this).

Your Bedroom

Your bedroom is a special place for you and your husband as a couple. Is that room as special as you would like it to be?

Think about function. What activities go on in the bedroom? Changing clothes, sleeping, making love, reading, folding clothes, doing paperwork ...

I don't think it's wrong to do other household activities in the bedroom, but I don't think they should detract from the atmosphere of the bedroom being a special place for the two of you.

If you fold your clothes on the bed, be sure that the clothes are put away promptly. If you do paperwork in the bedroom, sort and put away the papers. Are your craft materials taking over the bedroom? Buy some nice containers for storing projects or find another part of the house in which to be creative.

Make the bedroom a simple room that is conducive to intimacy, a place where you can talk, play, make love, and cuddle.

Practical thoughts ...

It's helpful to decide which activities will go on in the bedroom, and then remove anything not needed for those activities. Exceptions might be mementos or seasonal things stored in the closet.

Keep decorating simple. It's easier to keep clean and gives the room a more peaceful atmosphere. Clutter or lots of decorating "frou frou" can make the room feel distracting or chaotic.

Make the bedroom welcoming. Think comfort and function. "Pretty" is nice, but if your husband can't just fall down on the bed and has no place to put his pocket contents, he's not likely to feel welcome in his own room. I understand that this calls for a creative union between "pretty" and "practical," but it will be worth the effort when you wind up with a room that makes you both feel welcome and comfortable.

SUNDAY   MARCH 18
-♡-

Pray for your husband to have great favor at his place of work and that he will be seen as an asset to his company.

MONDAY   MARCH 19
-♡-

Leave a tender, silly, or sexy love note where he will find it (his reading book, lunch bag, or toolbox?).

TUESDAY   MARCH 20
-♡-

Let him choose. Whether it's the movie you're going to see or the kind of pizza you're going to order, let him make the choice today.

Loyalty in little things is a great thing.
Anonymous

WEDNESDAY   MARCH 21

-♡-

Ask your husband a few questions like "What is the sexiest thing I have ever done?" "What do you think is sexy?" and/or "What is not sexy to you?" Listen and learn.

THURSDAY   MARCH 22

-♡-

Make your husband's transition from work to home as peaceful and pleasant as possible. Take a little time to tidy up the living room. Give your kids a bit of attention, so that they don't rush dad the minute he walks in the door. Turn off the TV and put on some soft music. Don't bring up any stressful issues until he's had a chance to relax. Do whatever you feel will make your home a welcome respite after a long day at work.

FRIDAY   MARCH 23

-♡-

Look around for a small, practical gift to give your husband. Lip balm? A replacement screwdriver? A back-up for the toiletry that he runs out of all the time?

SATURDAY   MARCH 24
-♡-

Send a special invitation to your husband for an
evening of pampering. Help him out of his work
clothes, gently scrub him all over, and wash his
hair. Warm his towel in the dryer and take your
time drying him off. Curl up, snuggle, and then
have a time of leisurely lovemaking. Then spend
the rest of the evening enjoying each other's
company (have a meal, watch a movie, snuggle
up with a good book, etc.).

SUNDAY   MARCH 25
-♡-

Pray for your husband to have a growing
understand of what it is to be a godly man,
husband, and father. Our culture is pretty rough
on guys, so help him out by praying over his
masculinity and masculine roles.

MONDAY   MARCH 26
-♡-

Give your husband three different kinds of kisses
today (light, teasing, silly, French, slow romantic,
"got to have you now," etc.).

TUESDAY   MARCH 27

Make it easy for your husband to have time with his friends. It's incredibly healthy to have good same sex friendships.

... there is a friend who sticks
closer than a brother.
Proverbs 18:24b

WEDNESDAY   MARCH 28

Tell your husband how much the sexuality that the two of you share means to you.

THURSDAY   MARCH 29

Buy or make a throw/afghan for his favorite napping spot. A soft throw pillow would be nice too.

FRIDAY   MARCH 30

Do you have a diary or a journal? Maybe you just like to write out your prayers or thoughts. Let your husband take a peek and get to know your heart.

♡♡♡♡♡

SATURDAY   MARCH 31

Give your husband an all over massage. Yes, I said ALL over.   There is something really incredible about this kind of touch.   It is a wonderful way of saying "I love you," "You turn me on," and "I want to bless you" all at the same time.

Warm a bottle of massage oil in hot water. Have him lay face down on a large towel. Rub all the tiredness and soreness out of his muscles starting at his neck and shoulders and working down to his feet. Then have him roll over and work your way back up the front. Finish by stroking his genitals as foreplay, moving to warm, relaxed lovemaking.

Massage

Massage can seem a bit intimidating at first. How do you do it? How hard do you rub? Am I doing this right?

A few basics ...

Most people like to use lotion with a massage (it feels nice and keeps the friction down). There are ready-made massage lotions you can buy or you can use any body lotion. Warm the lotion by floating the bottle in a bowl of hot water. Pour a small amount into your hands (rather than pouring directly onto his skin) and add more as needed to keep your hands moving easily over his skin.

You will want to have him lay on a towel so that the lotion doesn't get on your bed or carpet (depending on where you give the massage). You might also want to have a small pillow or two handy to make your husband comfortable.

Take your time and move from one section of his body to another. There is no real right or wrong way to bless your husband with massage.

You can use several hand movements. Try:

♥ moving your hands in a circular open palm
   movement
♥ knead with the heel of your hand
♥ rub with your thumbs or fingertips
♥ alternate striking with the side of your hands
   (like Karate chop motions)
♥ squeeze or roll parts of the body (like gently
   squeezing and rolling toes or fingers

Husbands love touch. Any touch will bless them.
Unless your husband has injuries, you can be
fairly confident that you cannot hurt him. Use
common sense and ask for feedback. Ask your
husband where he is tense or sore (usually the
neck and shoulder muscles). Ask him to let you
know what feels good and what doesn't.

How to make you own lotion ...

Try mixing 40% walnut oil and 60% safflower oil
(these are available at most grocery and health
food stores). You can add a few drops of scented
essential oils (NOT extracts!) such as peppermint,
orange, etc. (also available at health food stores.).
If you are concerned about skin reactions, do a
small test a day or so before doing a full
massage.

SUNDAY   APRIL 1

-♡-

Take a moment and go into your bedroom. Sit on the edge of your bed and ask God to talk to you about your marriage. Listen for His leading and direction. Then pray that your bedroom would be a place of emotional, physical, and spiritual oneness.

MONDAY   APRIL 2

-♡-

Is there a particular blouse your husband likes to see you wear? Maybe there's a pair of earrings or a necklace he really likes? Make a point of wearing these things just for him.

TUESDAY   APRIL 3

-♡-

Be honest with him. Now, this is not license to blast away with everything that you want to say to him.   This is about respecting him enough to speak the truth in love at reasonable times. Be sure to be honest about good and encouraging things as well as those difficult areas of disagreement.

... but speaking the truth in love ...
Ephesians 4:15a

WEDNESDAY   APRIL 4

-♡-

Humor can add a sweet dimension to the bedroom. Leave a funny card on his pillow or hand him a bunch of green M&M's (silly aphrodisiac) just before bedtime.

THURSDAY APRIL 5

Make a small book of coupons with a kindness theme (back rubs, help with projects, favorite dinners. etc.). Tie them up with a bow and leave them on his pillow.

♡♡♡♡♡

FRIDAY APRIL 6

Try a new restaurant together. If funds are tight, you could try a new kind of cuisine at home. The idea is to share a meal and try something new together.

♡♡♡♡♡

SATURDAY APRIL 7

Hide your husband's clothes while he is in the shower. Hold them for ransom (you could even write a cute ransom note describing what he needs to do to get his clothes back).

SUNDAY   APRIL 8
-♡-

Pray for your husband's ability to be a good
steward. We're talking about more than just
financial/material stewardship. Pray also about
his stewardship of time, talent, relationships,
energy, etc.

MONDAY   APRIL 9
-♡-

Ask your husband, "What is the most romantic
thing I've ever done for you?" His response will
tell you something of how he defines romance.
Use that info to create new romantic memories.

TUESDAY   APRIL 10
-♡-

Buy or make a "You're Special Today" plate. I
have seen plates that have these or similar words
on them. There are also kits that allow you to
decorate a plate (available at most craft stores).
Another option is to buy a very unusual plate. Let
the family know that getting this plate means

you're special. Use it for birthdays and other celebrations. Make sure that your husband gets his share of "special" days. After all, he is very special.

Cherish your human connections, your relationships with friends and family.
Barbara Bush

WEDNESDAY   APRIL 11

-♡-

Put "make love with your wife" or "9:00 p.m. - meeting with (your name) in the bedroom (or wherever)" on his day planner or honey-do list.

THURSDAY   APRIL 12

-♡-

Touch is comforting. Give your husband a hug or two or three or four or more.

FRIDAY   APRIL 13

-♡-

Start a collection together. Whether it's collecting PEZ candy dispensers or fine antique books, you'll have lots of good quality time together looking for collectables.

SATURDAY   APRIL 14

-♡-

The unexpected can really spice things up. Try interrupting casual activities (like reading the newspaper, surfing the channels, or general dawdling) with an invitation to a little love making. Guaranteed he won't mind the interruption.

SUNDAY   APRIL 15

-♡-

Pray for your husband's relationship with his mother. Whether she's easy to get along with or not, living or gone, your husband needs to be able to be at peace over his (present and past) relationship with her.

MONDAY   APRIL 16
-♡-

Buy a CD of romantic music or find a radio station that plays romantic music that the two of you like. Then use it to add a bit of romantic ambiance whenever you have a little time for the two of you.

If music be the food of love, play on ...
William Shakespeare

TUESDAY   APRIL 17
-♡-

Sometimes it's a challenge to see accurately the effects of what we do. What a sweet encouragement it is to tell your husband when he's blessed someone or had a beneficial effect on a situation.

WEDNESDAY   APRIL 18
-♡-

When you and your husband are in a somewhat private place (in the car, in a darkened theatre, etc.) let your fingers do a little discreet wandering to his private places.

THURSDAY   APRIL 19

-♡-

Let him sleep in undisturbed or encourage him to take a needed nap.

♡♡♡♡♡

FRIDAY   APRIL 20

-♡-

Connect with your husband first thing in the morning. Make it a pleasant time. Help him get ready if he's the kind who likes help. Speak encouragingly and kindly.

♡♡♡♡♡

SATURDAY   APRIL 21

-♡-

Start a pillow fight (or wrestling match). Make sure he wins - you are the prize.

Edification

(A gussied up way to say build him up!)

Building up your husband is a continual action. It isn't a one-time thing that you do and are done. It comes one "stone" at a time - a kind word here, a thoughtful gesture there - over the long haul of the marriage.

Take some time to look at your "build him up" attitudes. Do you value him? Do you show it? Think about your words and actions, and daily do a little to "build" love and acceptance in your marriage.

Therefore encourage one another,
and build up one another ...
1 Thessalonians 5:16a

SUNDAY   APRIL 22

-♡-

Pray that your husband would be protected against temptation. Pray against the blatant and subtle things that would pull him off-balance in his walk with the Lord.

No temptation has overtaken you but such as is common to man; and God is faithful, who will not allow you to be tempted beyond what you are able, but with the temptation will provide the way of escape also, that you may be able to endure it.
1 Corinthians 10:13

MONDAY   APRIL 23

-♡-

Give your husband a pet name. It can be silly, sweet, or sexy, but let him know that he is special to you in a personal way.

TUESDAY   APRIL 24

-♥-

Be careful to respect the privacy of your marriage. Don't share personal information with your family or friends unless you know it would not bother your husband. Use respectful words when you do share and have a good motive in sharing (bragging on your husband, sharing a problem with a trusted friend in order to get advice, etc.).

WEDNESDAY   APRIL 25

-♥-

Exercise! Really. Take a daily walk or learn a new sport. A number of recent studies have concluded that exercise has a good effect on several areas of a person's life including sexuality, effecting both arousal and overall sex drive.

THURSDAY   APRIL 26

-♥-

Spend the evening doing what your husband wants to do. Watch his favorite show, eat his favorite snack, or play his favorite game.

FRIDAY   APRIL 27
-♥-

Keep an eye on the comics and clip some of the funnier ones. Laminate them (or use contact paper to cover them) and slip them into his books for bookmarks or toss one into his lunch bag for a laugh.

♥♥♥♥♥

SATURDAY   APRIL 28
-♥-

Try to get away as a couple once every 2-3 months for a few days. Yes, I know there are a billion reasons why this is difficult, but as a couple, you need this one-on-one time. To cut the cost, take your own food and swap babysitting with a friend (you can even stay at home, just close the window shades and don't answer the phone).

Sleep late. Make love. Go see a movie. Go for a walk. Talk about important stuff. Talk about silly stuff. Kiss a lot. Reconnect.

SUNDAY   APRIL 29

Pray that your husband would have wisdom and discernment while at work.

♥♥♥♥♥

MONDAY   APRIL 30

Give your husband a hug and kiss for "no reason" (though a serious or silly reason works well too).

♥♥♥♥♥

TUESDAY   MAY 1

Does your husband have old photos scattered in the back of drawers or crammed into ratty old boxes? If he's saved them this long, it's probably because those bits of history still mean something to him. Take the time to help him fix them up in a nice album or two.

WEDNESDAY   MAY 2

-♥-

Call your husband at work. Tell him you have a question for him and if he gets it right he can have a bedroom wish fulfilled. Make the question moderately hard. If he guesses right, do your best to fulfill his wish. If he guesses wrong, tell him you'll call back tomorrow with another question.

THURSDAY   MAY 3

-♥-

It's a whole lot easier to bless your husband when you know what he likes. Get a small notebook for your purse and write down all his clothing sizes, hobbies, favorites, things that seem to bless him a lot, anything that he mentions wanting, etc. Then when you want to bless him, you will have a lot of ideas and information with which to work. New shirt? You know his favorite color! Book? Oh, yeah, he seemed interested in the book that his friend mentioned. Need a little something to say I love you? You know his favorite kind of candy. Leave a few pieces on his pillow. (This is a great idea for everyone you love and especially helpful around birthdays and Christmas.)

FRIDAY   MAY 4

-♡-

Practice saying, "I'm sorry" and make it easy for him to say, "I'm sorry" too.

Let your forbearing spirit be known to all men...
Philippians 4:5a

SATURDAY   MAY 5

-♡-

If you usually make love in the dark, try it with the lights on (or low lights). If it's usually in the light, try it in the dark.

A Shared Meal

There is something quite special about the time shared over food - good food, good atmosphere, and good conversation - a shared heart, a shared life.

There's a lot of room for creativity. Here are a few ideas to get you thinking.

Who:
♥ the two of you

Where:
♥ the dinner table (dress it up a bit or create a theme)
♥ another place in the house (a picnic in the family room floor, breakfast in bed, a shared snack on the back porch)
♥ the great outdoors (the backyard, nearby parks, country pastures, the beach)
♥ a restaurant (this can be anything from fast food to fancy restaurants, a new place or an old familiar favorite)
♥ misc. odd places (snacks in the theatre or in the car on a road trip)

When
♡ usual mealtimes
♡ snack time (midnight snacks are fun)
♡ any time

What:

♡ a sack or picnic lunch
♡ a barbecue
♡ a rich dessert
♡ his favorite meal
♡ cookies or bread fresh out of the oven
♡ a new cuisine
♡ a variety of desserts
♡ a vegetable platter with dips

How:

♡ as a normal part of your day
♡ by invitation
♡ as a suprise

Why:

♡ to celebrate
♡ to discuss plans or share your day
♡ to relax and take a break
♡ to try something new

SUNDAY   MAY 6

Pray for the healing of any emotional wounds that your husband might have.

MONDAY   MAY 7

Get or make a pretty box. Use it to save cards and letters that your husband gives you (I hope it goes without saying that you don't have any cards or letters from old boyfriends tucked away!).

TUESDAY   MAY 8

Take a little time and join him in one of his interests. Life gets busy and sometimes you just need to let him know that he matters and that you want to spend time with him.

WEDNESDAY   MAY 9

Buy a pair of sexy undies and wrap them up for your husband. Enclose a note that says you will be glad to model the undies for him later that day.

Leave the gift where he will find it during the day. For those who send their husbands off to work, you could tuck it in their briefcase, lunch bag, or leave it on the dashboard for him to find as he drives off. For those with husbands who work from home, leave it on his pillow or his work area. If you have children, tuck it someplace where he will find it and they won't.

We shall never know all the good that a simple smile can do.
Mother Teresa

THURSDAY   MAY 10
-♡-

Smile at him.

FRIDAY   MAY 11
-♡-

When was the last time you went on a picnic together? Try one outdoors, indoors, lunch, dinner or even breakfast. Give your options some thought and make it fun and creative.

SATURDAY   MAY 12

-♡-

When you know that you will have some time alone with your husband, put on an interesting piece of jewelry and nothing else! I'm sure he'll take the hint.

♡♡♡♡♡

SUNDAY   MAY 13

-♡-

Pray for a sense of honesty and openness in your marriage.

MONDAY   MAY 14

-♡-

Ask around (some newspapers have an "about town" feature) and find something of interest in your area (a museum, a musical event, or a natural wonder or park). Wander about holding hands and sharing the experience.

TUESDAY   MAY 15

-♡-

Education time! Run, don't walk, to your local Christian bookstore, library, or used bookstore (I've seen some good titles there too). Bless your spouse with the new marriage skills you learn from great books like *Building Your Mate's Self Esteem* by Dennis Rainey, *The Five Love Languages* by Gary Chapman, or *Fall in Love, Stay in Love* by Dr. Willard F. Harley.

WEDNESDAY   MAY 16

-♡-

Write out the letters A-Z on a piece of paper. Then assign each letter a number, symbol, or different letter. Use this "secret code" to write your husband a sexy note. Hand him the mysteriously coded note (with a mysterious smile, of course) and give him a clue as to where the decoding sheet can be found (brief case, under his pillow, to be delivered in the mail the next day, etc.).

Sghmj fdmdqntr!

To decode: take each letter and move forward one letter in the alphabet ~ "S" become "T" "g" becomes "h."

THURSDAY   MAY 17

Buy your husband a cute mug for his coffee. Not a coffee drinker? Then get him another kind of glass or cup. There are clip-ons for the car, heavy- bottomed glasses for the spill-prone, and a number of colorful, creative glasses just for fun.

FRIDAY   MAY 18

Write down five things that you would like to do during your life. Ask your husband to do the same and then share with each other. What can you do to help each other make those dreams come true?

***We create our future
by what we dream today.***
Anonymous

SATURDAY   MAY 19

Make small casual gestures with a sexual undertone until he can't stand it anymore and has

to do something about it. Gently stroke his back
as you walk past him, put your feet in his lap
during a relaxing evening (wiggle them a bit, of
course), in a restaurant booth, slide your hand
along the inside of his thigh under the tablecloth,
slowly eat an ice cream in front of him, etc.

♡♡♡♡♡

SUNDAY   MAY 20

Pray for your husband's priorities. It's easy to get
busy and let life run over the important things.
Pray that your husband would have clear
direction, good priorities, and the inner motivation
to follow through.

MONDAY   MAY 21

Let him know what a great guy he is. Give him a
fun award like "best hubby" or "greatest kisser."
You can create a paper certificate award (with
kissy stickers) or take an old trophy and tape his
name and reason for the award over the old info.

TUESDAY   MAY 22

Encourage your husband over an area of his life where he has struggles. His work? Personal issues? His thought life? A relationship? A bad habit?

♥♥♥♥♥

WEDNESDAY   MAY 23

Spend time cuddling. Get a porch swing or a small loveseat and put it to good use often.

♥♥♥♥♥

THURSDAY   MAY 24

As a kindness, do your husband's least favorite chore for him. It's so nice to have that occasional break, to come home, and find that it's already been done.

FRIDAY   MAY 25

-♡-

When was the last time you shared your thoughts with your husband ... concerns about the kids, what you've been reading lately, a fear, a dream, a hope?

SATURDAY   MAY 26

-♡-

If you have occasion to get up in the night, when you come back to bed, gently wake up your husband for a little middle of the night lovemaking.

My beloved is to me a pouch of myrrh
Which lies all night between my breasts.
Song of Songs 1:13

Forgiveness

Forgiveness can be terribly difficult in marriage. In such a close and personal relationship, any selfishness or carelessness can really hurt.

> **And when you stand praying, if you hold anything against anyone, forgive him, so that your Father in heaven may forgive you your sins.**
> Mark 11:25 NIV

However, the scriptures make it clear that whether we are facing a small or large hurt, we need to forgive. It frees us from the ugly feelings of anger and bitterness and gives us the opportunity to express real love, as Christ modeled for us.

Take a moment and ask God to reveal any anger or unforgiveness you may have toward your husband. Ask for God's help in forgiving him.

SUNDAY   MAY 27

-♡-

Pray for good communication between your husband and his father, and between your husband and his children.

MONDAY   MAY 28

-♡-

Embroider a romantic saying on the edge of your husband's pillowslip (for those who are creatively challenged, try writing with a permanent marker and add an iron on appliqué or two). You could write, "You make my heart sing," "I will always love you," or put some XX's and OO's on there for kisses and hugs.

TUESDAY   MAY 29

-♡-

Keep your word. When you tell your husband that you will do something (or not do something), follow through. He is important and when you keep your word to him, you are showing him respect.

WEDNESDAY   MAY 30

-♡-

Take a moment in your day and imagine a wonderful time of lovemaking with your husband. Then call him at work (make sure he's on break or has a free moment) and tell him what you've been thinking about.

THURSDAY   MAY 31

-♡-

The next time your husband starts a project, play "go fer." Be willing to hold the flashlight or "go fer" a screwdriver. Hold the board in place while he screws everything down or hand the tools down to him when he's scooting around under the car. You'll save him oodles of time and have some nice couple time too.

FRIDAY   JUNE 1

-♡-

Fix up those photo albums. I know, photo albums can be a very painful subject (I have a stack of hard-to-identify photos too), but remembering those happy times will build your relationship.

If your photos are in a real mess, start fresh with a new album and your latest set of photos (or a group of photos from a special occasion). Work through the rest of your photos a bit at a time.

Your lips drop sweetness
as the honeycomb, my bride ...
Song of Songs 4:11a NIV

SATURDAY   JUNE 2

-♡-

Have you ever tried covering your husband with kisses, literally? Start at the top and work down. You may not get the whole job done, but it will be fun trying.

SUNDAY   JUNE 3

-♡-

Pray for your husband to have a growing hunger for the things of God.

MONDAY   JUNE 4

Hold his hand when you're watching TV or sitting in church. Little physical gestures tell him that you love him and want to be with him.

TUESDAY   JUNE 5

Dress up the dinner table ~ put on a pretty table-cloth, set out a candle or two, or set out your "nice" dishes. Make your husband feel more appreciated by making your dinner time together a little more special.

*Excellence is to do a common thing
in an uncommon way.*
Booker T. Washington

WEDNESDAY   JUNE 6

-♡-

Ask your husband to share his favorite sexual memory of you. Then sometime soon try to recreate it for him.

THURSDAY   JUNE 7

-♡-

Make an "Oops!" box for your husband's car or office. Put in things like safety pins, needle and thread, a small tube of superglue, duct tape, and anything else that he can use when he needs to fix something.

FRIDAY   JUNE 8

-♡-

What did you do when you were first dating? As newlyweds? Did you hang out at a certain restaurant? Bookstore? Bowling alley? Why not do some of the things you used to do and enjoy them all over again.

SATURDAY   JUNE 9
-♡-

If you're concerned about frequency in your sexual life, get a small calendar (for your bedroom, desk, purse, or whatever will work for you) and put a little mark on the days when you and your husband are sexual. Sometimes it helps to see in black and white how frequently you have sex, and then you can make whatever changes seem appropriate.

Sexual Teasing

Teasing is one way of deeply blessing your husband. It shows an interest in building and meeting his expectations of sweet things to come. Be sure to tease to a comfortable degree and always follow through (don't tease him and leave him sexually worked up for too long).

Basically, you want to do or say something that will tweak his sexual interest just a bit. If he can't do anything about it at the moment, all the better.

It will continue to build his interest for something later. Several tweaks will make his day or evening an exciting dance of erotic expectation.

Men are quite visual. Leave a button undone, flash a bit of thigh, leave your lingerie draped over his briefcase, or pull out the stops and do a long, slow dance for him (with or without clothes).

You can also use words to tantalize. This can be very effective in public (where no one else can hear your whispered words) or leave him sexy little notes, emails, or voice mail messages. Let him know what you like about him, what you want, and what you are going to do to him later.

Touch is another tweak tool. In public, you have to be a bit careful, but there are usually a number of opportunities during a given day when you can touch your husband in erotic ways. Give him a long kiss before dinner. As possible, stroke different parts of his body (you can even stretch or stroke yourself erotically when he's looking at you). By bedtime, he'll be dragging you off to the bedroom!

Take the time to reach out to your husband in sensual ways. Get him nicely worked up and then make an opportunity later to pleasure him fully.

SUNDAY   JUNE 10

-♡-

Pray for the atmosphere at your husband's place of work. Pray for peace and harmony in work place relationships. Pray for calm heads and patient attitudes.

MONDAY   JUNE 11

-♡-

If someone were to observe you and your husband, would they think you were in love? Regardless of the answer, take some time to evaluate (and change appropriately) how you treat your husband in public. Do you sit next to him, hold his hand, tease/flirt with him, or kiss him affectionately?

TUESDAY   JUNE 12

-♡-

Declare Husband Appreciation Day! You could mark it on his calendar or send an email announcing the event. Present him with a framed award declaring what a wonderful husband he is and how much you appreciate him.

WEDNESDAY   JUNE 13

-♡-

Write a romantic/erotic story with you and your husband as the characters. Make it believable and true to character, but use the story to sound out new and creative sensual experiences. Your husband will enjoy the story and maybe take a note or two.

♡♡♡♡♡

THURSDAY   JUNE 14

-♡-

Try to determine when there are times of stress in your husband's life and help take off some of the pressure. If you know Thursdays are rough at work, make sure that the house is quiet when he comes home and that you have dinner ready, or suggest a hot bath and a massage. If there's an up coming family reunion and you know that it's likely to be stressful, let your husband know that you are praying for him and that you can be signaled for "interference" if need be. Whatever his stress, look for ways to take off the edge.

FRIDAY   JUNE 15
-♡-

Research your family trees together. If that's not
desirable or possible, write about events that
have happened to the two of you. Write out dates
and interesting things and document your own
little bit of history making.

Every family tree produces some nuts.
Anonymous

SATURDAY   JUNE 16
-♡-

Make a "creative lovemaking" container. Gather
some slips of paper and ask your husband to help
you write out different things that you can try to
spice things up. Put them in the container and
when you are both feeling adventurous, pull one
out to try (be realistic in writing your ideas and
take into consideration your spouse's comfort
level).

SUNDAY   JUNE 17

-♡-

Unforgiveness is a heavy burden. Pray that your husband's heart would become soft and able to forgive those who have hurt him.

♡♡♡♡♡

MONDAY   JUNE 18

-♡-

Romance your husband with breakfast in bed.

♡♡♡♡♡

TUESDAY   JUNE 19

-♡-

The other day I saw a guy with MOG shirt. MOG? I thought. Well, upon closer examination I saw that it said "**Man Of G**od" in smaller print.

Why not get your husband a T-shirt that affirms his position in Christ or shows your love for him?

WEDNESDAY   JUNE 20

-♡-

Find a moment to talk to your husband about your sexuality. Share what you would like to see your bedroom life become. Ask him what he thinks. Are there things that he would like to do or not do? Are there things that you would like to do or not do? Do you need to change your priorities so that you have more energy and time for each other?

THURSDAY   JUNE 21

-♡-

Look for ways of showing small acts of kindness all day long. Pick up a plate, serve him a drink, rub his shoulders as you walk by, and let him know how thankful you are to have him as your husband.

FRIDAY   JUNE 22

-♡-

Plan a fun, casual outing. Do you like movies? How about the zoo? A walk around the park? Find something fun that you will both enjoy.

SATURDAY   JUNE 23

Try taking off a piece of clothing and dropping it on the ground. Then take a few steps and shed another item. Keep walking toward the bedroom (or wherever) dropping clothing as you go and see how long it takes to get his attention (if he's slow to catch on you can always ask for help with the bra clasp).

Attitude Check

I know, let's not go there, but really, our attitudes can greatly affect our relationships.

Sit for a moment and take an attitude check. How are you doing on patience, kindness, gentleness, and genuine thoughtfulness?

We all need to make attitude adjustments from time to time. Take that time now and ask God to help you grow in your ability to treat your husband with sweet attitudes.

SUNDAY   JUNE 24

Differences in gender, personality type, and life experience can make communicating a challenge. Pray for the ability to understand each other's differences.

MONDAY   JUNE 25

Sneak a fun picture of the two of you into his wallet. It never hurts to be reminded of those special moments of love and intimacy.

> ***How handsome you are, my beloved,***
> ***And so pleasant!***
> Song of Songs 1:16a

TUESDAY   JUNE 26

Compliment him every day for week. Need a little help? Think about how he looks, what he does or says, how he makes you feel, his abilities, or his character. Build him up by noticing those things that make him special and unique.

WEDNESDAY   JUNE 27

Spend a few days experimenting with different kinds of kissing. Give your husband a soft kiss when he gets home from work. Roll over and give him a silly kiss first thing in the morning and, of course, give him a long and sensuous kiss as he's leaving for work.

THURSDAY   JUNE 28

Does your husband frequently run out of certain things? Perhaps it's pens or computer paper. Shaving blades? His favorite kind of soap? Next time you're out, buy extra so that your husband has what he needs, when he needs it.

FRIDAY   JUNE 29

Try fixing a meal together. Fix pancakes for a weekend breakfast or make homemade pizza. Spend a little time together in the kitchen (if your husband really doesn't like working in the kitchen invite him to be your taste-tester).

SATURDAY   JUNE 30

Stretch your creativity a bit. Think of three different ways to invite your husband to have sex (and try them out on him over the next week). For example, there is the, "honey, could you help me with this curtain rod" (or other appropriate excuse to get him into the bedroom). There is also the direct approach, "Honey, you have on too many clothes." You could also send him a written invitation or leave a message on his voice mail.

Only conduct yourselves in a manner
Worthy of the gospel of Christ ...
Philippians1:27a

SUNDAY   JULY 1

Pray for your husband's sense of integrity. The world makes it easy to lie, cheat, and generally let your sense of right and wrong slide. Pray that God's way would be his way.

MONDAY   JULY 2

-♡-

Buy a white board marker or two (they come in all colors so get creative) and write a sexy message on your bathroom mirror for your husband. It's fun and an easy cleanup too.

TUESDAY   JULY 3

-♡-

We all need to be heard and respected. Remember to seek out your husband's opinion from time to time. Ask him what he thinks. Ask for ideas and solutions to problems that you face.

WEDNESDAY   JULY 4

-♡-

Femininity is an illusive quality, but certainly a quality that causes our husbands sit up and take notice. Take a moment and consider your clothes, movements, voice, and attitudes. What can you do to express your femininity more? If you are brave, you might talk to your husband about his views on femininity. If you are really brave, you might personalize it and ask him what you could do to be more feminine.

THURSDAY   JULY 5
-♡-

Make a conscious effort to give your husband your full attention several times during the day. When he walks in the room, set down what you're doing and speak graciously and kindly (a hug or kiss wouldn't come amiss).

FRIDAY   JULY 6
-♡-

Become his secret pal for a week (or a month). Send him a nice card in the mail, have his favorite lunch delivered to his work, or leave a little written prayer tucked under his windshield wiper. At the end of the week, take him to lunch and reveal yourself.

SATURDAY   JULY 7
-♡-

Never underestimate the excitement or pleasure of a "quickie." We think that because they are short and often hurried that they will be less fulfilling sexually. I suppose as a steady diet, they would be, but as the occasional treat, they can add an unexpected and delightful dimension to a couple's love life. Try having a quickie before work, during a commercial break, or anytime you have just a couple moments of privacy.

SUNDAY   JULY 8

-♡-

Pray for your husband's fellowship with other believers (whether he is a believer or not). Everyone needs good godly friends to hang out with.

His lips are lilies,
Dripping with liquid myrrh.
Song of Songs 5:13b

MONDAY   JULY 9

-♡-

Look for private moments to kiss your husband. In an elevator, in the car, passing in the hallway ... anytime you find yourself alone with him, take a moment to kiss.

TUESDAY   JULY 10

-♡-

Give special attention to the things that matter to him. Frame his awards, dust off his collection of pens, or create more space on a shelf for his new hobby or interest. Show him in a tangible way that what is important to him is important to you as well.

♡♡♡♡♡

WEDNESDAY   JULY 11

-♡-

Make your bed a place of touching, talking, snuggling, and making love. Try to keep all disagreements and tough discussions off the bed and in another room, or perhaps on a loveseat in the bedroom. Let your marriage bed be a place of blessing and intimacy.

THURSDAY   JULY 12

-♡-

Buy him a gift certificate to his favorite store or restaurant.

FRIDAY   JULY 13

-♡-

List all the reasons you are a better person for knowing your husband, and then find a quiet moment in your day to share them with him.

SATURDAY   JULY 14

-♡-

When you know your husband is interested in making love, ask him to lie down and then tell him that he can't move, on his honor. Then nicely take advantage of him. Take your time and really pleasure him and yourself too. You might have to remind him a couple of times that he can't move or you might find all rules going out the window (but that would be ok too).

Date Your Mate

To have a growing marriage you need to invest time and energy in the relationship. Don't expect your husband to do all the work when it comes to planning dates, do a little creative planning of your own.

♥ Dates can revolve around meals, interests, sports, or whatever sounds fun to the both of you

♥ Dates can be
    simple to extravagant
    free to major bucks
    spontaneous to well-planned

♥ Be on the lookout for moments that you can turn into a date. You can turn an errand into a mini- date by stopping for a quick burger (be sure to refill his drink and offer warm conversation) or you can turn a lazy Saturday afternoon into a movie date (rent a movie and pop some popcorn).

♥ Are there interests that you have in common? If you both love dogs, keep an eye out for a dog show. Do you both enjoy art or music? The newspaper will have a listing of events in your area. Wherever there is an interest, there are opportunities to have fun investigating that interest.

♡ Use dates to celebrate promotions and achievements.

♡ Plan a date during a busy season just to connect with your husband.

♡ Celebrate holidays (you can create your own nonsensical holidays if you need an excuse).

♡♡♡♡♡

SUNDAY   JULY 15
-♡-

Pray for your husband's sexuality. The world offers a lot of garbage, both in teaching and in temptation. Pray for him to have a balanced, healthy sexuality that he can joyfully share with you.

Let marriage be held in honor among all ...
Hebrews 13:4a

MONDAY   JULY 16
-♡-

Leave a sweet or romantic message on his voice mail or answering machine.

TUESDAY   JULY 17
-♡-

When you are out and about with your husband, be sure to let him know how much you enjoy spending time with him.

WEDNESDAY   JULY 18
-♡-

Buy a clear shower curtain. (For those of us who are on the shy side, realize that men really do enjoy their wife's body. They don't see all the imperfection that we are aware of, they just love to see their beloved. Be generous and let him see what he adores.)

THURSDAY   JULY 19
-♡-

When you're headed out to the store, take a moment, and ask your husband if there's something that he wants that you can pick up for him. You'd be amazed at what caring about a simple desire will do.

FRIDAY   JULY 20

-♡-

Pray for and find another couple (perhaps from your neighborhood or church) that can be friends with you and your spouse. Plan and prepare for a fun night in your home. Eat, talk, laugh, and play games. Share a great time with your husband in the presence of friends that you hold in common.

> *I cannot even imagine where I would be today were it not for that handful of friends who have given me a heart full of joy. Let's face it, friends make life a lot more fun.*
> Chuck Swindoll

SATURDAY   JULY 21

-♡-

Invite your husband to undress you (it's even nicer if you're wearing something with lots of buttons or layers - anticipation, you know).

SUNDAY   JULY 22

-♡-

Pray for your husband's ability to be faithful and creative at work.

MONDAY   JULY 23

-♡-

Invite your husband to go somewhere new. Where haven't you gone?   What haven't you done? Try a new adventure altogether.

TUESDAY   JULY 24

-♡-

Make or buy him a bookmark that has an encouraging thought or scripture.

The excellence of a gift lies in its appropriateness rather than in its value.
Charles Dudley Warner

WEDNESDAY   JULY 25

Find three different ways to tell your husband that he's sexy (and you don't necessarily have to use words). Some ideas - give him "that look," give him your secret "I love you" signal, tuck a sexy card into his lunch sack, whistle at him, pat or stroke your favorite spot, and ... oh yeah, you can just tell him outright that he's your idea of one really bodacious hunk of sexy man.

THURSDAY   JULY 26

Give his tired feet a rub down (after a shower, if you need to).

FRIDAY   JULY 27
-♡-

Go along with a smile. Yes, I know baseball can be terribly boring, and we don't even want to talk about golf. However, for the sake of relationship, you might want to consider stifling those yawns and, instead, find a little something that you can enjoy about his favorite pastime. Join him in what he enjoys doing and give it a chance. That smile you brought along might come in handy as you enjoy the day with your favorite friend.

SATURDAY   JULY 28
-♡-

Invite your husband to a private indoor picnic where the rule is - no clothing allowed. Spread a comfy blanket (a few pillows are nice too) and set out an assortment of goodies. When he asks for dessert, let him know that you're it!

Kindness

I looked up the word "kind" in a dictionary.
It said:

♡♡♡♡♡

♡ of a friendly, generous, and warm-hearted nature

♡ considerate, forbearing, tolerant, agreeable, understanding, charitable, showing sympathy

♡ desiring to promote the welfare or happiness of another

♡♡♡♡♡

Yeow! That's a tall order. I used to think that something like this was an impossibly high standard, but more and more I am convinced that with little daily expressions of romantic, practical, intimate, and thoughtful love, we can live with our husbands as kind and thoughtful lovers. Kindness is not out of our reach, it is just daily baby steps away.

SUNDAY   JULY 29

Pray that your husband would have a sense of joy and peace as he goes through his day.

MONDAY   JULY 30

Give him 365 (one for everyday of the year) chocolate kisses (Hershey's chocolate candies) with a note about how much his kisses mean to you or how he should never be without your kisses.

TUESDAY   JULY 31

Make a point of telling your husband any good news first, and then share with the rest of the world. He'll know that he's first in your book.

No act of kindness, no matter
how small, is ever wasted.
Aesop
(from The Lion and the Mouse)

WEDNESDAY   AUGUST 1

Baby him a little. After a long day at work, help him undress, bathe/shower (take your time) and dry him off. Then spend some time combing his hair and rubbing any tired muscles with a nice lotion (kisses help too).

THURSDAY   AUGUST 2

When your husband faces a mess, be kind and step in to help him clean it up. Whether it's a paperwork mix-up, spilled punch, or a messy garage, smile, roll up your sleeves and be a help.

FRIDAY   AUGUST 3

Look around and see if you can find a class to take together - a language class, ballroom dancing, or a Bible study (in a pinch you could read and study the same book). Look at your common interests or try something altogether new.

SATURDAY   AUGUST 4

There are always those one or two positions that a couple falls into for sex, because they are known and comfortable. Just to make things interesting, consider suggesting a new position. If you need ideas, there are books that use sketches instead of photos (*A Celebration of Sex* by Dr. Douglas E. Rosenau is one of them).

SUNDAY   AUGUST 5

Every marriage needs fun and laughter. Pray for the entertainment and recreational time you spend with your husband.

MONDAY   AUGUST 6

Do something romantic in rhyme. If you are gifted enough that you can write your own romantic poems, go for it! If not, check out a book of poetry from the library (or grab one off the shelf if you are the literary type) and pick out a poem that really speaks your heart.

TUESDAY   AUGUST 7

-♡-

When was the last time that you messed up? How would you like to have been treated? With kind words, forgiveness, and understanding? With scolding, complaining, or faultfinding? That's a no-brainer, right?

How do you treat your husband when he messes up?

... forgive and comfort him
... reaffirm your love for him.
2 Corinthians 2:7-8

WEDNESDAY   AUGUST 8

-♡-

Leave a negligee or a pair of sexy undies on the edge of the bed or draped over the bedroom chair. The idea is that you are tweaking his mind a bit. You are giving him a visual reminder that you are sexual and that you want him.

THURSDAY   AUGUST 9

-♥-

When you know that your husband is having a hard day, offer to run interference for him so that he can have some space. We all need a little peace and quiet, now and then.

FRIDAY   AUGUST 10

-♥-

Buy him something fun, like a pen with wiggly eyes, a package of stickers, a fishing lure (or other appropriate hobby item), or his favorite kind of candy.

SATURDAY   AUGUST 11

-♥-

A part of keeping things interesting is being able to surprise your husband from time to time. Make a sudden sexual move when it's not expected, by either stroking "interesting places" on him or taking his hand and placing it on your "interesting places."

Taking an Interest in Him

We all want to be noticed and appreciated. So love on your husband by taking an interest in him and his interests, involvements, and dreams.

Be sure and take a little time each day to ask about his day. At other times, encourage him to share his dreams or his concerns about his work.

You can take any of this a step further and get involved. Help with a project at his work, join him in his daily jog, or pray and work with him toward fulfilling a dream.

Love him by being interested and involved in his life.

SUNDAY   AUGUST 12

Pray for your husband's "love walk." Nothing reveals the heart of God like the expression of love, and as ambassadors for Christ we all need the ability to love as He loved (for those with unbelieving spouses, pray that your husband would see God's heart revealed in your "love walk").

Love is patient, love is kind,
and is not jealous;

love does not brag and is not
arrogant, does not act unbecomingly;

it does not seek its own, is not provoked,
does not take into account a wrong suffered,

does not rejoice in unrighteousness,
but rejoices with the truth;

bears all things, believes all things,
hopes all things, endures all things.

Love never fails ...
1 Corinthians 13:4-8a

MONDAY   AUGUST 13

-♡-

Declare "Kiss Day" and take every opportunity to kiss him. Kiss him when you wake up, when you walk by him, when he leaves for work, when he comes out of the shower ...

TUESDAY   AUGUST 14

-♡-

Take a moment and pick up the house before he gets home. It's nice to be treated with that kind of thoughtfulness and respect.

WEDNESDAY   AUGUST 15

-♡-

Spend a day in the nude with your husband - clean house, watch TV, read, whatever. If you have kids, you might try making your bedroom a no clothes zone. Whatever your circumstances, think skin. It's an incredible intimacy builder because your husband is the only one that sees that much of you.

THURSDAY   AUGUST 16
-♡-

Buy your husband some men's vitamins.

FRIDAY   AUGUST 17
-♡-

Share your past. When something brings up a memory, take the time to share that memory with your husband. He's a part of your present and your future. Share the past with him too.

Drink and imbibe deeply, O lovers.
Song of Songs 5:1b

SATURDAY   AUGUST 18
-♡-

Give your husband permission to enjoy physical intimacy with you anytime. Whether it's a hug, a caress, intercourse, or a long snuggle, choose to be warm and available. It's an incredible gift to know that physical touch and intimacy will be warmly received.

SUNDAY   AUGUST 19
-♡-

Mentoring is God's way of passing on wisdom and experience. Does your husband have a mentor or is he a mentor to others? Pray for those relationships.

MONDAY   AUGUST 20
-♡-

Just before you are going to see your husband (he's getting off work, you're meeting him for lunch, whenever), take a moment and "pretty up." Comb your hair, freshen your makeup, or put on that piece of jewelry he loves. Let him know that he's your favorite guy and you want to look good for him.

TUESDAY   AUGUST 21
-♡-

Find a place or an activity that you save just for your husband. Maybe there's a restaurant that is your special place or perhaps you go to flea markets with him on the first Saturday of the month. Find some special place or activity that is reserved for him alone.

WEDNESDAY   AUGUST 22

I saw the cutest pillow. It said "Tonight!" on it. If you can't find one ready made you could get sew on or iron on letters to create your own.

THURSDAY   AUGUST 23

Clip articles of interest to him. Whether it's about his favorite hobby or about work related interests, help him gather that needed or wanted info.

But the fruit of the Spirit is love, joy, peace, patience, kindness, goodness, faithfulness, gentleness, self-control ...
Galatians 5:22-23

FRIDAY   AUGUST 24

-♡-

Take some time out to watch a TV program with your husband, something that will be of interest to him. If he's into science, watch NOVA. If its sports he likes, join him in watching a game (don't forget a few munchies and toss in a little hand holding). If you are a no-TV household, look at the stars or sit on the porch and watch the passers-by.

♡♡♡♡♡

SATURDAY   AUGUST 25

-♡-

Play an old-fashioned game of hide and seek with a new twist. Nonchalantly walk up to your husband and hand him your undies. Let him know you want to play hide and seek, tell him to cover his eyes and count to 20 (on his honor) and then tuck yourself into a really good hiding place (scout out your house during the day for a good spot). Then delight him when he finds you.

Notes

Notes can be a fun tool for blessing your husband. They offer so many creative ways to reach out to him and share your love and appreciation.

They can be used to

- ♡ encourage him when he's down or facing a challenge
- ♡ excite and entice him
- ♡ amuse him and give his day a lift with humor
- ♡ thank him for something he has done
- ♡ share some good news
- ♡ communicate love and appreciation

SUNDAY   AUGUST 26

-♡-

Pray for your husband's prayer life. Pray that he would be drawn to spend time talking to God.

MONDAY   AUGUST 27

-♡-

Plan a surprise getaway for the two of you. It doesn't have to be expensive. You could plan a lunch picnic at a nearby park or pull out the stops and plan a little vacation, motel and all. You could go to a free showing at a local museum or get tickets to something you both enjoy. The idea is to surprise him with a little special time just for the two of you.

TUESDAY   AUGUST 28

-♡-

Spend time just listening to your husband. If he's not much of a talker, "listen" to his body language. Become a student of your husband's thoughts and moods.

WEDNESDAY   AUGUST 29

-♡-

Kiss in the dark. Whether it's a darkened theatre or an evening moment on the back porch, snuggle up in the dark for a moment of sweet intimacy.

THURSDAY   AUGUST 30

-♡-

Give your husband a good old-fashioned back scratch.

FRIDAY   AUGUST 31

-♡-

When was the last time you spent a lazy day with your husband? Read the paper in bed, snuggle, talk, rent and watch a movie, go for a walk, dream, and enjoy each other's company.

SATURDAY   SEPTEMBER 1

-♡-

One way of showing warmth and receptivity is to be more vocal during lovemaking.

SUNDAY   SEPTEMBER 2

-♡-

Pray for your husband to be a blessing to customers at work. Pray that he would be encouraging, helpful, kind, and patient.

MONDAY   SEPTEMBER 3

-♡-

Frame the lyrics to your favorite love song or scripture and hang it in your bedroom.

TUESDAY   SEPTEMBER 4

-♡-

Send your husband an encouraging email at work. "I'm praying for you," or "you bless me," are good themes.

Anxiety in the heart of a man weighs it down, but a good word makes it glad.
Proverbs 12:25

WEDNESDAY   SEPTEMBER 5

-♡-

When you are having a quiet moment with your husband, run your fingers lightly over his face or hands. Gently move over the contours and stroke every feature or finger.

> *His head is like gold, pure gold; ...*
> *His hands are rods of gold set with beryl ...*
> 'Song of Songs 5:11a,14a

THURSDAY   SEPTEMBER 6

-♡-

Take a little time and fix up the car. Clean it up a bit and put a couple of nice things in it, like music tapes, decent cup holders, an organizer for important car info, or a cool scripture on safety. Make sure that the trunk has a good working jack, a few simple tools, and whatever else will make breakdowns easier to handle. Then take a moment and pray over the car, for the general condition of the car, traveling safety, and for blessed conversations during driving.

FRIDAY   SEPTEMBER 7

-♥-

Develop a common interest; perhaps a new sport or maybe a new area of study. You could work puzzles or work with wood. Build some activities in your lives that will give you the opportunity to spend time together.

SATURDAY   SEPTEMBER 8

-♥-

Look through your clothes and jewelry (or buy something new) for an item to use as a signal to your husband. When you wear it, you are interested in a little bedroom play.

♥♥♥♥♥

SUNDAY   SEPTEMBER 9

-♥-

Men tend to hold things in. Pray for hidden stresses and fears that your husband may be struggling with (work, money, health, etc.).

MONDAY   SEPTEMBER 10

-♥-

When was the last time you told your husband that he has beautiful eyes or cute dimples? Look at your husband and compliment him on some part of his physical appearance.

TUESDAY   SEPTEMBER 11

-♥-

You know how you have ideas and a general plan about how things should go? Well, your husband has ideas and plans too. Take the time to hear him out and then value his opinion enough to push some of those ideas into reality.

...let the wife ... respect her husband.
Ephesians 5:33b

WEDNESDAY   SEPTEMBER 12

Think about sex during the day (if you have to, leave yourself little reminders around the house - like heart stickers).

I know that sounds a bit funny, but for a lot of women it's hard to make the jump to being sexual after a long, busy, and non-sexual kind of day (diapers and dishes are not aphrodisiacs). If you think about sex (and maybe even plan for it) during the day, it will be easier to be interested and available later.

♡♡♡♡♡

THURSDAY   SEPTEMBER 13

Your husband likes his friends for a reason. He enjoys their company. I know we all love to have our husbands to ourselves, but just as a kindness, include your husband's friends at a dinner or event from time to time.

FRIDAY   SEPTEMBER 14
-♡-

Buy a new game and give it to your husband wrapped up as a gift. Include a card with an invitation to play.

SATURDAY   SEPTEMBER 15
-♡-

Greet him at the door in some pretty lingerie (make that the bedroom door if you have kids).

*You have made my heart beat faster with a single glance of your eyes, with a single strand of your necklace ...
the fragrance of your garments is like the fragrance of Lebanon.*
Song of Songs 4:9b,11b

Compliments

Isn't it nice when someone compliments you on something you have done well? It's wonderful to be appreciated and it's helpful to get some feedback on what you do with your time and energy.

It's the same way for your husband. He needs to be told often about how he is appreciated.

Compliment him on:

♡ his appearance (this includes new clothes or a new haircut, as well as those cute dimples that you love)

♡ his character (has he been honest or generous, has he shown integrity?)

♡ his handling of a tough situation

♡ his use of natural talent and abilities

SUNDAY   SEPTEMBER 16

-♡-

Pray for a sense of oneness and unity of purpose between you and your husband. Pray about the things that build you as a couple and over those things that tend to separate the two of you or cause division.

MONDAY   SEPTEMBER 17

-♡-

Put on some slow romantic music and invite your husband to slow dance with you. Be sure to give him a few slow romantic kisses too.

TUESDAY   SEPTEMBER 18

-♡-

Does your husband have a spot in the house that is "his space"? Without interfering, make sure that it is clean and that he has what he needs for that space. A comfy afghan and pillow for his favorite couch? Something to put his reading material in? Maybe a coaster for a drink or a small shelf for his favorite memorabilia?

WEDNESDAY   SEPTEMBER 19

-♡-

Take your husband shopping with you. No, really!
Just be sure to stop in the undies section and let
him pick out something that he would like to see
on you.

... she provides food for her family ...
Proverbs 31:15 NIV

THURSDAY   SEPTEMBER 20

-♡-

Fix up several single servings of his favorite foods
and put them in the freezer. Then when you're
sick, busy, or off on a woman's retreat, he can
easily have his favorite foods.

FRIDAY   SEPTEMBER 21
-♥-

Send your husband a funny card or e-card.

Laughter is the closest distance between two people.
Victor Borge

SATURDAY   SEPTEMBER 22
-♥-

Guys want to be wanted too. So when the opportunity arises, say something really direct, like "I want you now!" or "Why aren't you naked?"

SUNDAY   SEPTEMBER 23
-♥-

Pray for your husband's speech, that it would be full of blessing, kindness, and truth.

MONDAY   SEPTEMBER 24
-♡-

Ask your husband what kinds of things communicate love to him? Is it kisses? Home cooked meals? Fresh warm towels after a bath? Find out, and then make a point of communicating that kind of love often.

TUESDAY   SEPTEMBER 25
-♡-

When you and your husband have a disagreement, take some time to really listen. Try to understand his perspective. Many times it's possible to do something a number of ways. It may be that his perspective is not wrong; it's just another possible way of doing something.

WEDNESDAY   SEPTEMBER 26
-♡-

Buy him some nice "manly" lotion. Offer to help him with his back, feet, or wherever. Baby him a little and make it a nice sensual experience.

THURSDAY   SEPTEMBER 27

Encourage him to take care of himself. Is he getting enough sleep? Good food? Personal time (recreation, hobbies and interests)? Do what you can to help.

♡♡♡♡♡

FRIDAY   SEPTEMBER 28

Volunteer together. Whether it's donating blood or helping out at the local food bank, do something of worth together.

♡♡♡♡♡

SATURDAY   SEPTEMBER 29

Play Esther for a day. Take the time to soak in the tub. Soften rough spots with lotion and spritz on his favorite scent. Pick out your prettiest outfit and fix your hair. Meet your husband at the door and make him feel like a king.

The Kid Krunch

Kids are lovable and wonderful. Without them we wouldn't experience the magical joy of Christmas morning or the mystery of fireflies and tadpoles.

But in a very practical sense, children can put the crunch on your couple time. They are more immediately needy (try ignoring a tired three year old or two children in the throes of sibling rivalry), and there is always the pull to spend as much time as you can with them because you have them for such a short time (they really do grow up overnight). I'm all for spending lots and lots of time with your children, but that time needs to be balanced with your personal and marriage needs.

Taking time for your husband and building a strong marriage is not selfish. It is beneficial for everyone. It keeps your marriage healthy for a lifetime, which in turn helps your children feel more secure, gives them good role models for marriage, and develops in them a healthier sense of self.

Give plenty of time to those wiggly little bundles of puppy dog tails and sugar and spice, but, please, make regular time for your very important man.

SUNDAY   SEPTEMBER 30

-♡-

Pray for the circumstances and people that cause or have caused your husband grief, pain, or shame. Pray for emotional healing and the restoration of relationships.

MONDAY   OCTOBER 1

-♡-

When you are out and about, make a quick stop for ice cream cones as a mini-date.

TUESDAY   OCTOBER 2

-♡-

Fix his favorite meal.

WEDNESDAY   OCTOBER 3

-♡-

A really fun thing to do, that builds intimacy within a marriage, is to develop hand signals for private messages. Lightly scratching the back of his hand can mean, "I'm tired, do you mind if we leave?" or tugging at your earlobe can mean, "I will always love you" or "meet you in the bedroom." Be creative and have fun with this one.

THURSDAY   OCTOBER 4

Find a moment to slip up behind your husband and give him a little shoulder and neck rub. This is always an appreciated gesture, especially at the end of the day.

A cheerful heart is good medicine ...
Proverbs 17:22a NIV

FRIDAY   OCTOBER 5

Spend time with your husband watching a really funny movie or telling jokes.

SATURDAY   OCTOBER 6

A man's sexuality can be greatly affected by what he sees. Try putting a mirror or some mirror tiles by the bed.

SUNDAY   OCTOBER 7

Pray that your husband would have a desire to know God's truth about his life. Sometimes it's easier just to believe what you are taught or what people think about you. It takes courage to seek truth and walk in it, but it's just that kind of truth seeking that will set him free to be the man of God that he was designed to be.

If you abide in My word, then you are truly disciples of Mine; and you shall know the truth, and the truth shall make you free.
John 8:31b-32

MONDAY OCTOBER 8

Next time you fix him a sandwich, trim it to look like a heart. Other food items might lend themselves to this creative art, a slice of meatloaf or other cut of meat can be trimmed a bit, as can slices of cake or soft cookies.

TUESDAY OCTOBER 9

Your husband's a good man, right? Now, 'fess up. He's done a lot of helpful and generous things and over time you've taken that for granted. Well, stop that. Go in there and thank him for all those little things that he usually does without thanks or notice (like filling the gas tank or picking up when you're tired).

WEDNESDAY OCTOBER 10

Sleep naked. There's something very warm and special about skin on skin and it's guaranteed to keep the fire burning (if you have kids put a robe by your bed).

THURSDAY   OCTOBER 11

-♡-

Everyone gets behind now and then. When life throws you a curve, you tend to drop the less significant things to take care of the more important things. When you see your husband getting swamped by circumstances, give him a helping hand - perhaps wash, wax, and vacuum his car or straighten up the garage or tool shed, whatever he drops. Doing something like this can show him that you care, that you understand that he's a little swamped, and you want to bless him.

FRIDAY   OCTOBER 12

-♡-

Share a little piece of your heart by taking your husband to your favorite spot and sharing it with him.

SATURDAY   OCTOBER 13

-♡-

Give your husband three bedroom wishes. You have the right to refuse on the grounds of discomfort, etc, but do your best to fulfill his dreams.

Sexuality

Boy, howdy, this is a tough topic to talk about. There are so many confusing sexual messages that we hear from family, society, and the church, and it's such a personal topic.

Let me just say that God designed sex to be a wonderful part of marriage. When we run from or don't explore that area of our marriage, we shortchange both our spouses and ourselves. We weaken the very fabric of our marriages.

God designed us to find pleasure in our sexuality. He even gave us a special organ just for sexual enjoyment. The clitoris has no other purpose. Our sexuality is not dirty or bad. It is remarkably wonderful. God called our design "very good" and gave us sex as a wonderful wedding gift.

Sex is there to be the glue in your marriage. It's the one thing that you do with your spouse that you don't (or shouldn't) do with anyone else. It makes you one physically and bonds you emotionally and spiritually.

I do understand that many women struggle with accepting and enjoying their sexuality. I encourage you to make this a matter of prayer and study. Challenge yourself to know what God says about sex and your sexuality. Prayerfully work to grow in this area so that you and your husband can enjoy this wonderful gift often and joyously.

♡♡♡♡♡

SUNDAY   OCTOBER 14

Pray that your husband would have favor with his co-workers and that he would be a blessing to them.

MONDAY   OCTOBER 15

Sticky notes are really great when it comes to romantic messages. You can leave a trail of sticky notes. You can cover a pillow in sticky notes. You can leave them in fun and interesting places that he'll find today or maybe tomorrow.

Take a trip to your local office supply store and check out their selection of sticky notes. Buy a few and have some romantic fun.

TUESDAY   OCTOBER 16
-♡-

Be tolerant of his quirks. I realize that some guys are quirkier than others (I know I married one), but understanding his unique idiosyncrasies and personal likes and dislikes show that you care about and respect him as an individual.

WEDNESDAY   OCTOBER 17
-♡-

Now, don't take this personally. Make a habit of regularly brushing your teeth and keep some mints or flavored candies by the bed or in your purse. A fresh, sweet kiss is a wonderful invitation.

THURSDAY   OCTOBER 18

Help him with those things over which he struggles. Does he hate to shop for clothes? Maybe he just loses his mind when it comes to buying gifts for friends at the office. Whatever his struggle is, help him out.

*Love is not only something you feel.
It's something you do.*
David Wilkerson

FRIDAY   OCTOBER 19

Buy your husband something that complements his hobby or interests. It doesn't have to be expensive, a magazine or other small item will do. Just let him know that you think of him and want to bless him.

SATURDAY   **OCTOBER 20**

-♡-

Make love to all of his body. It's easy to get in a rut and go through the same few motions during sex. Instead, take time to stroke, kiss, or nibble his ear, the back of his leg, the small of his back or all of his fingers (or toes).

SUNDAY   **OCTOBER 21**

-♡-

Pray for your husband to feel loved and accepted (that is the heart cry of us all). We can show our love, but sometimes it takes prayer to get it down into our husband's heart.

♡♡♡♡♡

MONDAY   **OCTOBER 22**

-♡-

Kiss your husband in 10 different places. Have fun with this!

*Courtesies of a small and trivial character
are the ones which strike deepest
in the grateful and appreciating heart.*
Henry Clay

TUESDAY   OCTOBER 23
-♡-

Take the time to show him common courtesies.
Say please and thank you. Listen to him when he
speaks and respond pleasantly. Let him know
that you hear him and that he matters to you.

WEDNESDAY   OCTOBER 24
-♡-

Read a good book on sexuality (if your husband is
willing, read it with him). I recommend *Sheet
Music* by Dr. Kevin Leman and *A Celebration of
Sex* by Dr. Douglas E. Rosenau.

THURSDAY   OCTOBER 25

-♡-

Keep an ear open for those things that your husband mentions that he would like, whether it's a book or a new tool. Then make a point of buying it for him and leave it wrapped up where he'll find it.

FRIDAY   OCTOBER 26

-♡-

Share with your husband what you have been studying or praying about. Talk about your thoughts and feelings and about how what you've been studying is affecting your life and what you believe.

SATURDAY   OCTOBER 27

-♡-

Is your husband a couch potato? Preempt his TV time by commandeering the couch before he gets there (wearing something provocative, of course). You can do the same thing with the chair at his computer or the stool at his hobby workbench.

Conversation

(Something to talk about!)

I think it's perfectly fine to talk about the kids, the housework, and whatever is a normal part of your day. However, I think it's equally important to expand your world by taking an interest in other things. Not only will it make your life a little more fun, it will open the door to creative conversation with your husband. If you're the talkative type, it will give your husband some variety in what he hears from you. If you are the quiet type, it will help you hold up your end of any conversation.

A few ideas …

♥ watch the news

♥ read a good book (the Bible, a classic, a book of famous quotations, or a fun novel)

♥ learn about a topic (your family's history, eagles, or wild flowers)

♥ study something (art, your city's history, or child development)

SUNDAY   OCTOBER 28

-♡-

God gave married couples the gift of sex. Pray for passion in your marriage.

MONDAY   OCTOBER 29

-♡-

Remember that skirt or that necklace that he likes so much? Make a point of wearing them just for him.

You have made my heart beat faster...
With a single strand of your necklace.
Song of Songs 4:9b

TUESDAY   OCTOBER 30

-♡-

Reserve an evening or weekend to do just what he wants to do. Life gets busy and sometimes you just need to take the time to let him know that he matters and that you want to spend time with him.

WEDNESDAY   OCTOBER 31

-♡-

Get something sheer. Our husbands are very visual. They love to see their beloved. So buy (or make) something sheer - a nightie, a small robe, or an over-jacket (even if it covers regular clothing, the sheer quality will be a nice touch).

♡♡♡♡♡

THURSDAY   NOVEMBER 1

-♡-

Put on his favorite music when he comes home for the day (if he's an at-home worker, put it on when you know he would appreciate it).

FRIDAY   NOVEMBER 2

-♡-

What does your husband like to do with his spare time? Invite him to join you in doing just that. Tennis? Watching movies? Scrounging through flea markets? Whatever it is, just do it.

O my dove ...
Let me see your form,
Let me hear your voice;
For your voice is sweet,
And your form is lovely.
Song of Songs 2:14

SATURDAY   NOVEMBER 3

-♡-

Invite your husband to play a card game with you. After you deal, tell him the rules have changed! It's now *strip* UNO or even *strip* "Go Fish.

This means that when certain hands are played the player has to lose an item of clothing or put one back on. For example, every time someone has to "draw 4" in UNO, they have to remove something or when they lay down a set in "Go Fish" they can retrieve an item. Have fun making up the rules. It's silly fun and, in general, you are not expected to finish out the game.

SUNDAY   NOVEMBER 4

-♡-

Take some time to pray for your husband's study time. Pray for clarity and new insight. If your husband is an unbeliever, pray over whatever he does during "quiet time," whether it is reading, gardening, or just daydreaming. It is during those quiet times that the Lord can snag their hearts and minds, and effect real change and growth.

MONDAY   NOVEMBER 5

-♡-

When was the last time that the two of you had a nice quiet candlelit dinner? If you can't afford a dinner out, fix his favorite meal and set out a couple candles of your own.

TUESDAY   NOVEMBER 6

-♡-

Celebrate his milestones (both large and small - new job, personal accomplishment, etc.) with a special meal, silly framed award (as appropriate) or other acknowledgement.

WEDNESDAY   NOVEMBER 7

Get a small journal and keep a record of your romantic/sexual relations. Researchers have done a number of studies on folks doing this and it has been known to have beneficial results. It helps to give a more accurate picture of your sexuality and it helps people focus on and build a healthier sexuality.

THURSDAY   NOVEMBER 8

Serve up your husband's favorite dessert. It's those little things that make him feel special.

***The way to a man's heart
is through his stomach.***
Anonymous

FRIDAY   NOVEMBER 9

Plan and throw a party together. It can be small or large, but enjoy the fun of planning something together and having a good time with your friends and/or family.

SATURDAY   NOVEMBER 10

Create an invitation to sex. I mean an actual piece of paper in an envelope that invites your husband to make love with you (like an invitation to your own private party). You can word it any way you like, put little stickers on it, and/or scent the paper. Just have fun with this and make your husband feel special.

♡♡♡♡♡

Holidays

Priorities

Perhaps the best gift any wife can give her husband is that of being the "unfrazzled wife" during the holiday season. I know, I'd like to have perfect presents for everyone, a beautifully decorated home and yard, and mounds of homemade cookies as far as the eye can see, but let's be reasonable. We are only human and we have a limited amount of time and energy that we can give to those special days. We need to be organized, be willing to simplify, and do the things that mean the most to our families and ourselves. We need to save enough of our own time and energy to actually enjoy the season and be warm spouses and (relatively) calm parents (I've had to clean up spilled gravy and assemble toys too!).

Don't be afraid to limit your engagements, simplify your meals, or tone down your gift giving.

A practical suggestion:

♡ Get a notebook for keeping holiday info. Write down everything that you would like to do, circle the really important stuff, and then cut back on the rest or cross it off your list altogether. Use the rest of the pages in your notebook to write out in simple do-able terms how to accomplish your holiday plans. (See page 202 for an online help for organizing and preparing for the holidays.) You can write out gift ideas and keep an eye out for sales during the year. You can make notes about simple decorating ideas to use this year or next. You can bake ahead and freeze breads and cookies. It doesn't all have to be done during the holiday season. Most of the planning and much of the work can be done during the year.

Traditions

Traditions are a huge part of the holidays. They remind us of special times and connect us to the people we love. In planning for your holidays you may want to ask family members what traditions are especially important to them (you could have a time of sharing memories around the dinner table and ask each about their favorite traditions). Yes, that might mean you will have to fix that "unique" cranberry relish that Grandma Ethel used to make, or you might have to sing a carol or two, but isn't that what the holidays are about?

You may also wish to create new traditions as a couple or as a family. There are any number of volunteer organizations that would love help. There are yearly events to enjoy. You might even want to start a holiday collection of plates or tree ornaments. (Paul and I give each of our children an ornament every year. When they are grown, they get to take their ornaments with them for their own tree.)

Be willing to let go of traditions that have little meaning to your family in favor of the traditions that really bless your family.

Extended Family and Friends (the good, the bad, and the wonderful)

With extended families, blended families, and a host of friends, it can be a real challenge to deal with all the opportunities to celebrate. Take some time to talk with your husband about where and with whom you will be spending your holidays.

Parents (and other challenging relatives) - It is certainly kind to honor your parents and bless them over the holidays, but at the same time you and your husband did "leave and cleave" and you need to do what is wise and best for the two of you (and any kiddos). Prayerfully consider how best to spend a reasonable amount of time with any extended family and still have the energy you need to spend the holidays in a way that will bless you, your husband, and your immediate family.

♥ Create a couple of private hand signals to use at gatherings. Use them to signal, "Help!" when you are cornered by Great Uncle Henry, or "I'm tired, can we work toward leaving?" Don't forget the "you look sexy" or "I can't wait to get you home" signal.

♥ Look for opportunities to compliment your husband in front of family and be sure to refill his drink and get him some munchies

♥ Do your best to be a peacemaker. Yes, I know your husband's ex has made life "interesting." Just don't bring her up, and change the subject as soon as you can if someone else brings her up. No, you shouldn't scream and throw things at Aunt Sarah. Yes, I know she hugs way too much and her chatter drives you nuts. She probably needs attention and appreciation (don't we all). Tell her how lovely she looks in her new dress and then excuse yourself to help in the kitchen. Family peace really is important. You can sow kindness and caring, honestly you can. (I'm not talking about a truly abusive situation here. When any abuse cannot be controlled or limited, be willing to gently, but firmly stand up for your family and/or walk away.)

Blended Families

Visitation can be very challenging during the holiday times. Please work to make the holidays as joyful and low-stress as possible for your children, even if that means a bit of creative shuffling or giving up a party or event. Kids of divorce hurt considerably over the loss of their original family, and often feel guilty when they visit their other parent. Do what you can to give them as much comfort and as little hassle as possible.

Sometimes the kindest thing you can do is to play by the rules and make whatever time you have with your children relaxing and comfortable. You may not have Thanksgiving or Christmas day with them, but you can bless them greatly by not complaining about the inconvenience or airing hurt feelings. Yes, I do understand that many situations will not be fair, but it's not fair for your kids either, and they need love and consideration from you, the parent. Make the best of any bad deal and cover everything in prayer.

♡♡♡♡♡

Friends

They enrich our lives so much, but this is another area where you and your husband will have to consider your level of involvement. Select a few important (to you) events or throw a party of your own. Perhaps plan to have drinks/snacks and small gifts for friends who drop in.

Pray also at this time for safety as family and friends are traveling to different homes and events. Pray for family hurts (we all have them). Pray for a spirit of peace over your husband and household.

Just the Two of You

Do make time over the holidays for just the two of you. Create your own personal traditions (kiss every night at the same time or go to an afternoon movie every Christmas Eve). Plan at least one simple date to connect with your spouse. Put a small touch of holiday fun in your bedroom (a couple of candles or a string of lights?) and be sure to share holiday flavors with a kiss (peppermints are fun!).

♡♡♡♡♡

Practical help

Check with your husband to see what batteries you need for holiday gifts, and then buy what you need plus a few so that you have a nice supply on hand. Pick up any holiday loose ends for your husband. Errands? Something to return?

Ask your husband if you can help him with choosing and purchasing gifts. He may need gifts for friends or co-workers. Even buying for family members can be tough. Be available to brain storm for ideas and do a little running around for him.

SUNDAY   NOVEMBER 11
-♡-

Pray for your husband's relationships with his extended family - both his family and yours.

... so far as it depends on you, be at peace with all men
Romans 12:18

MONDAY   NOVEMBER 12
-♡-

Get some pictures taken of the two of you. If a portrait studio package is going to break the budget, have a friend take a couple of rolls of pictures of the two of you. Pick out the best ones to frame or make a special album.

TUESDAY   NOVEMBER 13

-♡-

Does your husband have a dream? What can you do or say to encourage that dream? Perhaps you could buy him a how-to book about it. Maybe you could write him an encouraging note, "I know God will help you reach your dream!"

WEDNESDAY   NOVEMBER 14

-♡-

Next time you hear your husband in the shower, quickly shed your clothes and join him. Make it a nice sensual experience and be sure to baby him a bit, wash his hair, scrub his back, etc.

THURSDAY   NOVEMBER 15

-♡-

From time to time, ask your husband if there are errands that you can run for him. If you ask on a day that you are doing errands, you can run them all together. It will save him time and not add too much to your day.

FRIDAY   **NOVEMBER 16**

-♡-

Find a quiet moment in your day to share what is happening in your life - your concerns, your hopes, any good news, and things you are struggling with.

SATURDAY   **NOVEMBER 17**

-♡-

Think "sneak attack." When can you catch your husband off guard for a quick little romp in the bedroom?

SUNDAY   **NOVEMBER 18**

-♡-

Pray for your husband's recreation time. We all need to relax and enjoy ourselves from time to time. Is he getting enough playtime? Does he have good, healthy things to do? Are there forms of recreation that you can join him in?

MONDAY   NOVEMBER 19
-♡-

Buy a small journal or notebook and write something romantic in it. It might be something as simple as, "I love you." Leave it out on his nightstand where he will find it and from time to time add other writings, a scripture, a quote, heart stickers, a photo, whatever. It will become an ongoing reminder of how much you love him.

TUESDAY   NOVEMBER 20
-♡-

We all make mistakes and act with occasional selfishness. When your husband falters, be quick to forgive.

WEDNESDAY   NOVEMBER 21
-♡-

Add some romantic lighting to your bedroom. Good ideas are candles and oil lamps (watch where you place them) or lights with dimmer controls (you can buy dimmers to attach to existing lamps at any hardware store). Mirrors can reflect lighting for an interesting effect.

THURSDAY   NOVEMBER 22

Remember to buy his favorite munchies when you go shopping. It's those thoughtful little actions that tell him you care.

FRIDAY   NOVEMBER 23

Whatever you have or whatever you are doing, offer to share with your husband. Share your ice cream cone, share a sunset, or share the remote control to the TV.

And do not forget to do good
and to share with others ...
Hebrews 13:16a NIV

SATURDAY   NOVEMBER 24

Meet your husband as he steps out of the shower with a warm towel (toss it in the dryer for a minute or two) and a warm embrace (no clothes allowed).

SUNDAY   NOVEMBER 25
-♡-

Pray for your husband's relationships at work. Pray for his ability to communicate with his boss and co-workers and generally get along with them.

MONDAY   NOVEMBER 26
-♡-

Try a new flavored lip gloss and ask your husband how he likes the flavor.

TUESDAY   NOVEMBER 27
-♡-

Do something the way he likes it done. Whether it's putting the toilet roll on "backwards" or fixing chicken his favorite way, show him that he matters by considering his likes.

WEDNESDAY   NOVEMBER 28
-♡-

Serve dinner wearing only an apron (this may take a little planning if you need a kid-free evening or if you need to put up some extra curtains).

THURSDAY   NOVEMBER 29

Keep the candy jar on his desk filled. If he's on a diet, make it sugar free candies.

FRIDAY   NOVEMBER 30

Play the memory game. Take turns asking, "Do you remember the time we ..."

SATURDAY   DECEMBER 1

Get a pad of sticky notes (like Post-It notes) and put on some lipstick. Use fairly dark lipstick and put kiss prints on a number of the sticky notes. Place a note in a fairly noticeable place with a little helpful clue or arrow that points to the next sticky note. Leave a fun trail of "kissy" notes that ends with you (complete with a real warm and inviting kiss).

Gift Giving

I recommend starting with prayer (I'm really not being facetious). Some men are tough to buy gifts for and finding something meaningful can be a true challenge. A thoughtful gift or two blesses the receiver. Price or number of gifts is of lesser importance.

Here are some gift giving suggestions ...

Buy a small notebook to record his preferences and interests. What is his favorite color? What are his hobbies? Does he have a favorite sports team? Would he appreciate a homemade gift? Does he like personalized items? Monograms? Also write out his clothing sizes and any kind of information that you think you might need (like he's missing a 3/4" wrench).

Listen to what he talks about for clues to what he might like. For example, if he likes a particular Ansel Adams photo, look for an AA calendar or perhaps a coffee table book of his pictures.

Look at how he spends his free time. What are his interests and activities? Then look for items that will compliment his interests.

Consider item gifts (a basketball), activity gifts (tickets to a game), and service gifts (coupon to do his least favorite chore).

Remember to give him something that he likes, rather than something that you want him to like.

A few ideas to brainstorm over ...

Reading
♡ a book that he has mentioned wanting
♡ a book by his favorite author
♡ books/magazines about his favorite interests
♡ membership in a book or reading club
♡ a gift certificate to his favorite bookstore
♡ bookplates
♡ a bookmark
♡ bookends

Car Stuff
♡ jumper cables
♡ "Fix-it-Flat" (the big one with the hose)
♡ latex gloves or towelettes with cleaner in them
♡ a small tool kit for the trunk
♡ a new tape or CD
♡ a cup holder that really works
♡ a pouch for important car papers
♡ a flashlight
♡ a first aid kit

♥ a seat pad
♥ hand lotion, tissue, and other travel toiletries

Clothes
♥ socks
♥ a tie
♥ mittens, gloves, or a hat
♥ sunglasses
♥ fun print boxers (Sponge Bob? Scooby Doo?)
♥ new shoe laces for his tennis shoes
♥ shoe polish or shoe care kit
♥ belt or suspenders

Cooking/Grilling
♥ an apron
♥ mitts or hot pads
♥ cooking or grilling tools
♥ a chef's hat
♥ recipe books/magazines

Food
♥ bake up a batch of his favorite cookies
♥ a coupon good for his favorite meal
♥ create a gift basket of fun or exotic foods

Games
♥ a new game
♥ books/magazines on his favorite game
♥ game equipment (like a new chess set)
♥ computer game software

Gardening
♥ gardening tools
♥ gardening tool organizer/container
♥ a hose reel
♥ a garden journal (notebook for recording garden activity)
♥ gardening books/magazines
♥ garden/landscape design software

Hobby related gifts - for an existing hobby or perhaps to start a new one
♥ books/magazines on the hobby of choice
♥ hobby materials (like coin sleeves for the coin collector)

Jewelry
♥ rings
♥ tie tacks
♥ cuff links
♥ fun pins
♥ a watch

Just for Fun
♥ a kite or other childhood toy
♥ a lava lamp
♥ his favorite candy

Personal Items
♥ any item that he tends to run out of (be sure to get his favorite style or brand)

♥ a new wallet
♥ "manly" stationary/notes, include some stamps
♥ a journal with a great looking pen
♥ framed photos
♥ camera and film

Relaxing Time
♥ an arm chair caddy for the TV remote
♥ new earphones for his sound system
♥ a tape or CD by his favorite artist
♥ an afghan/throw for his favorite napping spot
♥ a pillow for the same spot

Sports
♥ a cushion for bleachers
♥ sports books/magazines
♥ tickets to a game
♥ coupon good for munchies and drinks during
   the Super Bowl

Work or Desk
♥ a briefcase
♥ a business card holder or container
♥ desk organizers
♥ a calendar

If you are still struggling a bit, invite a couple of friends to brainstorm with you for ideas.

On the flip side of the coin, when it comes to gifts that you receive from your husband, be sure to show your appreciation for any gift he gives you. Even if it is ... um ... unusual. Your husband put thought, time, effort, and money into your gift. To accept his gift is to accept him. Love the gift because he gave it to you as an expression of his love and appreciation.

Gratitude is the most exquisite form of courtesy.
Jacques Maritain

You can minimize the possibility of "unusual" gifts by being clear about what you would like. When you are out with your husband, pick up or point to things that you would enjoy receiving. He's not a mind reader. Be kind and help him out.

SUNDAY   DECEMBER 2

Pray for your husband's perception of himself. It's so easy to live out the life script that others have written for you, being who others say you are. It's far better to know who you really are in Christ and who He designed you to be. It's an out-of-the-box move, but, oh, what a difference!

MONDAY   DECEMBER 3

Learn to say, "I love you" in a foreign language. Here are a few choices. A library book or an online search will give you plenty more options.

Chinese: Wo ie ni.
French: Je T'aime.
German: Ich liebe dich.
Italian: Ti amo.
Klingon: Qabang!!!
Pig Latin: I ovelay ouyay.

TUESDAY   DECEMBER 4

-♡-

When you buy a new outfit, save it for a special time with him. Put on some nice makeup and fix your hair a bit. He's worth dressing up for.

WEDNESDAY   DECEMBER 5

-♡-

Buy a small basket (you might have something you could use around the house) and fill it with some massage oil (baby oil or body lotion will do in a pinch), massage roller (those cute little wooden roller things), and a couple of hand towels (for clean up). Pretty it up with a bow and leave it where your husband will find it.

THURSDAY   DECEMBER 6

-♡-

Give him the benefit of the doubt when there are misunderstandings. None of us is perfect when it comes to communication and mistakes will happen. Handle them with grace and kindness.

FRIDAY   DECEMBER 7
-♡-

When was the last time that you and your husband just did something around town? Look through your local newspaper and see what freebies are going on. Have a picnic while listening to the local orchestra's concert in the park. Wander through a new exhibit at a local museum. Have some "together time" as you explore what your city has to offer.

SATURDAY   DECEMBER 8
-♡-

Take some time to play with his senses. Run your fingers lightly over him, all over him, taking your time. Cover him with kisses or make a long, interesting trail of kisses. Or experiment with different textures (feathers, fur, silk or a soft paintbrush) against his skin. If he's adventurous, you can blindfold him and do any of the above.

SUNDAY   DECEMBER 9
-♡-

Pray for favor with your husband. A wife should have a special spot in her husband's heart. He should be able to love and cherish her. He should be able to be tender toward her. This may take time, forgiveness, healing, or simply the understanding that a wife needs this special position in his heart.

The heart of her husband trusts in her ...
Proverbs 31:11

MONDAY   DECEMBER 10
-♡-

Plan a double date with friends. You can have pizza and games at your house or share a meal at a nearby restaurant. Just enjoy being a couple and sharing the evening with friends that you both enjoy.

TUESDAY   DECEMBER 11
-♡-

Do you have a nice photo of your husband in your wallet? If not, find a shot that you like and put it in the *first* sleeve of your photo collection (be sure he sees it there).

WEDNESDAY   DECEMBER 12

-♡-

Have you ever told your husband that he is a good lover? Now would be a good time. Having trouble in the bedroom? Tell him one thing that he does in the bedroom that blesses you.

THURSDAY   DECEMBER 13

-♡-

Give your husband a little extra attention by giving him a manicure or pedicure.

FRIDAY   DECEMBER 14

-♡-

Take your husband out for a treat. Get two spoons and share a hot fudge sundae or get two straws and share a chocolate shake.

SATURDAY   DECEMBER 15

Semi-nudity can be as alluring as nudity, sometimes even more so. Try spending a couple of hours without a top on or wearing just a T-shirt. Sooner or later, it will have the desired effect on your husband.

♡♡♡♡♡

Kisses

Kisses are very important because they bring you face to face in an intimate way. Kisses are a precious reminder of the special relationship that you have with your spouse. Use this romantic tool to build plenty of intimacy in your marriage.

♡ Kiss often

♡ Kiss with different purposes (to comfort, to entice, to tease, etc.)

♡ Kiss creatively (give him a silly kiss, pass a small candy to him with a kiss, kiss every finger and toe, etc.)

SUNDAY   DECEMBER 16

-♡-

Our world is full of things that clamor for our attention. So, pray for your husband's thought life, that he would be consistently drawn to what is right and honorable

... whatever is true, whatever is honorable, whatever is right, whatever is of good repute, if there is any excellence and if anything worthy of praise, let your mind dwell on these things.
Philippians 4:8

MONDAY   DECEMBER 17

-♡-

Buy one of those tiny jigsaw puzzles. Put it together, flip it over, and write a romantic message on the back. Take it apart, put it back in the box, and put a pretty ribbon around it. Leave it where he will find it with a note - "I really flip over you, when you've solved the puzzle you can *FLIP OVER ME* too."

TUESDAY   DECEMBER 18

-♡-

Make a list of things that you like about your husband and leave it where he can find it.

WEDNESDAY   DECEMBER 19

-♡-

Sometime when you're just snuggling, take his hand and place it on your breast. It's an invitation to touch something that he loves touching anyway and you are giving him a not-so-subtle message that you are available and that you like his touch.

THURSDAY   DECEMBER 20

-♡-

Does your husband have enough room for all his "stuff"? Clean out the closet a bit and make more room for his clothes. Straighten up a corner of a room or a few drawers to make room for his hobby stuff. Look around the house to see how you can accommodate his physical space needs a little better.

FRIDAY   DECEMBER 21

Grab your husband and curl up somewhere private. Talk about your dreams and create a wish list of things that you would love to do together. Do you want to take a trip? Maybe you want to learn a language, retire early, or build a new home. What are your dreams? Share them and work to make them a reality.

A house is made of walls and beams,
a home is built with love and dreams.
Anonymous

SATURDAY   DECEMBER 22

Ask your husband for help with a project in another room and then "ambush" him for a little lovemaking.

SUNDAY   DECEMBER 23

-♡-

Pray for your husband's relationships with your children. Pray that he will be sensitive to them, make time for them, and really listen to them. Pray that he will understand the role that he needs to fulfill in their lives.

MONDAY   DECEMBER 24

-♡-

Call him at work just to say, "I love you."

TUESDAY   DECEMBER 25

-♡-

An integral part of building up your husband is reassuring him that he is needed. Let him know all the ways in which you need him (yes, this is an exercise in vulnerability).

WEDNESDAY   DECEMBER 26

-♡-

Let your husband know that you are not wearing undies on your way out to a party (a quiet word, a brief glimpse, or discreetly tuck your undies in his pocket).

THURSDAY   DECEMBER 27

-♡-

Pick up his socks (or deal with other disagreeable habit) without complaining. Then spend some time thanking God for your husband. List his strengths and all the good things that he does for you and the family. Ask God to give you patience and wisdom concerning his faults and to help you keep them in perspective with all the good that he does.

FRIDAY   DECEMBER 28

-♡-

Put a little gift on his pillow. It could be a new key ring, a chocolate sampler or a little love note. It's a small tangible way to tell him that you thought about him during the day and that you appreciate him.

SATURDAY   DECEMBER 29

You know what turns your husband on. So do it ~ and make it plain that you did it on purpose. In effect you are saying that you like his sexuality to the point that you enjoy deliberately turning him on.

SUNDAY   DECEMBER 30

Pray for your husband's safety - physically, emotionally, mentally, and spiritually.

MONDAY   DECEMBER 31

Give your husband a warm hug and whisper, "I love you," in his ear.

A note from Lori

So how are you doing? Have you been able to live out a few of the generous tips? Does your husband have a smile on his face? Do you?

I sincerely hope that you have been able to weave generosity into the fabric of your marriage. I encourage you to keep at it until being generous is a very natural part of your day. This investment in your marriage will result in a lifetime of happy memories and the gift of "no regrets."

Blessings, Lori <><

If you have questions or comments, I would be pleased to hear from you.
email: Lori@The-Generous-Wife.com

♡♡♡♡♡

Dear Father,

I pray for the reader of this book. Please help her to practice and live out generosity in her marriage. Help her to personalize her giving and caring. Help her to understand her husband and find ways of loving him that will bless him and build intimacy in their marriage.

Father, please soften the heart of her husband toward her. Help him to open up to her generosity and caring. Build trust and caring between them.

In Jesus' name I pray. Amen.

Good Books

Building Your Marriage

The Five Love Languages
by Gary Chapman

Building Your Mate's Self-Esteem
by Dennis Rainey

Staying Close
by Dennis Rainey

Married Sexuality

Intimate Issues
by Linda Dillow and Lorraine Pintus

Pillow Talk
by Karen Scalf Linamen

Sheet Music
by Dr. Kevin Leman

A Celebration of Sex
by Dr. Douglas E. Rosenau

Prayer Power

The Power of a Praying Wife
by Stormie Omartian

Understanding Your Man

Making Sense of the Men in Your Life
by Dr. Kevin Leman

Personality Plus
by Florence Littauer

After Every Wedding Comes a Marriage
by Florence Littauer

The Proper Care and Feeding of Husbands
by Dr. Laura Schlessenger

Woman Power
by Dr. Laura Schlessenger

For more book suggestions see The Generous
Wife bookstore.
http://the-generous-wife.com/books.shtml

Online Resources

ORGANIZING FOR THE HOLIDAYS

Holiday Grand Plan
http://organizedchristmas.com

MARRIAGE COUNSELING

American Association of Christian Counselors
http://aacc.net

MARRIAGE RESOURCES

The Generous Wife website
http://www.the-generous-wife.com

The Generous Husband website
http://www.the-generous-husband.com

The Marriage Bed
http://www.themarriagebed.com
(This site has articles on sexuality from biblical and scientific perspectives. Public bulletin board for discussion.)

Book 22
http://www.book22.com
(This site sells intimacy products for married couples. Christian, discreet, no nudity, no mailing list.)

For more online resources see The Generous Wife links page.
http://the-generous-wife.com/sites.shtml

About the Author

Lori Byerly is a marriage minister and co-creator of The Marriage Bed. She ministers online, writing materials for The Marriage Bed and The Generous Wife sites.

She and her generous husband have been married for 20 years. They live in Austin, Texas and have a daughter and son

Printed in the United States
23707LVS00003B/3

9 780971 804043